A Year with
Rudolf Nureyev

A Year
with
Rudolf Nureyev

Simon Robinson
with
Derek Robinson

ROBERT HALE · LONDON

ISBN 0 7090 6102 1

Robert Hale Limited
Clerkenwell House
Clerkenwell Green
London EC1R 0HT

2 4 6 8 10 9 7 5 3 1

Photoset in North Wales by
Derek Doyle & Associates, Mold, Flintshire.
Printed in Great Britain by
St Edmundsbury Press Limited, Bury St Edmunds
and bound by
WBC Book Manufacturers Limited, Bridgend.

Contents

List of Illustrations   7

  1 Crossed Paths   11
  2 Strictly Professional   17
  3 Short Intermission   23
  4 Cleveland, Ohio: A Slap on the Ass   27
  5 The Dakota: 'Fifty grand for a pair of buns'   35
  6 La Scala: The *Nutcracker* Olympics   47
  7 Paris: 'You shout, I won't cry'   55
  8 St Barts: Margot Calling Long-distance and
     Jackie for Tea   65
  9 The Dakota Again: 'Nev mind dat'   97
 10 Britain: 'What sort of shit town is Harrogate?'   109
 11 Verona: 'A quick, short kick on the backside'   123
 12 Li Galli: 'Foof! Too slow'   129
 13 Vienna: More Than a Famous Name   145
 14 Stormy Weather: Food, the KGB and
     Bedtime Rituals   153
 15 Only One Way Out   165
Index   173

Illustrations

1 Rudolf signing every last autograph during his British tour

2 Dancers thanking Nureyev after the last night of the British tour

3 Rudolf with friends after the final performance of the British tour, in Brighton, 18 May 1991

4 The airstrip at St Barts

5 Rudolf's beach-front house on St Barts

6 On St Barts with Rudolf

7 Rudolf, after breakfast, on St Barts

8 With Rudolf and the car he couldn't drive!

9 Rudolf and Bach on St Barts

10 Rudolf eating lunch outside on a rare occasion when he is without his shawl

11 Grand Saline, the nudist beach on St Barts

12 Rudolf's seafront place on St Barts

13 Rudolf with Uros Lajovic and Papa Hubener

14 Rudolf at his very best having fun on his motorbike

15 Rudolf easing into his new career with Wilhelm (Papa) Hubener, Elisabeth Hubener, Ilse Wincor and Howard Penny

16 Rudolf's Mediterranean island of Li Galli

17 Rudolf's bath on Li Galli

Illustrations

18 On the boat from Li Galli to Capri

19 Sharing a joke and a little day music on Li Galli with Howard Penny

20 Rudolf after we went to a dinner party on Capri

21 Rudolf wearing a rich robe for a photo-shoot on Li Galli

22 Rudolf looking like a medieval monarch!

23 The multi-million-dollar feet

24 One of many pairs of Rudolf Nureyev's practice shoes

25 Chichi, the dog, on Li Galli, sheltering beneath some of Nureyev's costly fabrics

26 Rudolf's $50,000 Greek statue

27 Rudolf rehearsing an outdoor concert at Ravello

28 The dining-room at Nureyev's Manhattan apartment

29 Rehearsing *L'après-midi d'un faune* in an outdoor arena near Amalfi

30 The dining-room in the Paris apartment with some examples of Nureyev's taste in paintings

31 Rudolf's richly furnished lounge in Paris revealing his great talent as a collector

32 Works of art in the Paris apartment

To Jane, for waiting

1

Crossed Paths

I first met him in 1989. By then Nureyev had made himself the greatest male dancer of the century, perhaps of all time. In 1989 he was fifty-one, long past the age when most dancers quit. Nureyev never quit. He worked to the end of his life. When his body could not dance he learned to conduct – not ballet scores, but symphonies. Nureyev had colossal drive, enormous vitality. Part of that drive and vitality expressed itself, unforgettably, in dance. Another part expressed itself in sex. Long before I met him he had been sexually self-indulgent on a huge scale, a homosexual Don Juan. The tragedy of Nureyev is that he could never be satisfied; he always hungered for more. On-stage, that hunger created genius. Off-stage, eventually it killed the genius.

But to the very end he put the utmost into life, and he got the most out of himself, and out of others. That was heroic. He never let failure enter his plans. That was heroic. And when the sickness corroding his once magnificent body could not be ignored, he never complained; he worked even harder. That was heroic.

11

Nureyev crossed my path, quite literally, one dark and rainy night on the island of Saint Barthélemy, which everyone calls St Barts. It's in the Caribbean. We were both heading for *La Banane*, probably the best restaurant on the island. I was the mate on an ocean-going yacht that was visiting the island. And I wouldn't have been there if a teenage girl hadn't attacked the woman I was working for in London and cracked her skull. Life can be very unpredictable.

I grew up on the island of Jersey, which is a good place to learn to sail. Plenty of people own yachts and they like to race or cruise them in the English Channel. They need keen young men to grind winches and run out spinnakers and so on. I was an expert crewman when I was still a teenager. Then I discovered tall ships, and I crewed on the *Sir Winston Churchill* for three trips.

Tall ships are indeed tall. The masts of the *Sir Winston Churchill* reach 115 feet above the waterline, but going aloft was always pure pleasure. Next I went to Kathmandu because it sounded romantic and exotic. I wasn't prepared for filth, poverty, disease and child mutilation. All very sobering. I came back to Jersey and began work in childcare. This led to a job with Barnardo's in London. I thought I'd found my career. Within twelve months I was suffering burn-out. It was lucky my injuries weren't more permanent.

This Barnardo's was a school for adolescent girls. They'd all been damaged: rejected, or injured, or abused. The staff were excellent, and needed to be. The girls had every reason to be angry at the world. There were riots and fights, screaming and swearing. One night I arrived to start my shift and found a fourteen-year-old girl sitting on an upstairs window ledge and holding a razor-blade to her wrist; she was waiting to spray blood over the first staff member to appear below. So it was a tough job. One day, during a routine meeting, a girl attacked my supervisor and cracked her skull. Worse things had happened, but I couldn't shake off the shock of that incident. 'Three years in childcare is a long time,' my boss said. 'Maybe you need a break.' Simultaneously, an old friend asked me to crew on his yacht in a fun race to the Caribbean. I took a sabbatical and went. It was November 1988.

A year later I was still in the Caribbean and still sailing, but I'd worked my way up to being the mate on a big, fast, high-performance yacht, *Ocean Leopard*. My job was to run the deck. This can be a hazardous place when a boat like *Ocean Leopard* is racing (as she often was when we were chartered). The sails are huge and the sheets (or ropes) to secure them can be an inch and a half thick – yet at times they jump about like snakes. Get one around your wrist at the wrong moment and it will cut your hand off. The sheets pass through steel blocks that travel along steel tracks set into the deck. If somebody's foot gets caught in a track, it might be painful. All this on a sloping, heaving, slippery deck, with the crew trying to change a sail the size of a tennis court. Winning the race was important, but making sure that no guest got hurt was crucial. When I got the job, the skipper told me that if I could handle it, in a year *Ocean Leopard* might be mine – as skipper. A cheerful prospect for a lad not yet twenty-six. And I was getting good money.

In December 1989, we sailed from Antigua to St Barts for a charter inspired by the Beaujolais Nouveau Run. In our case the wine was *rosé* and the guests were *vignerons* – owners of vineyards in the south of France. Next day we took part in the *Route de Rosé*, a not-too-serious race around St Barts. We had several cases of *rosé* on board. And Rudolf Nureyev.

It rained heavily, early on the night before the race. We all went to dinner at *La Banane*: the *vignerons* and their wives and girlfriends, the skipper and the crew. As our car drove slowly into the restaurant car-park, the headlights swung, briefly picked out a man walking alone, and then lost him. I recognized him at once. To which you might say: Who wouldn't? But his was the last face anyone would expect to see in a Caribbean car-park on a wet December night; and in any case I knew almost nothing about ballet, had never seen him before and wasn't even sure he was alive. All I got was a glimpse of a man very strangely dressed.

Despite the rain, the evening was warm; most of the crew were in shorts and polo shirts. Nureyev wore long, wide trousers, a big flowing shawl over his shoulders and a beret. So it must have been his face that grabbed my attention. (It had that effect on people. When I worked for him I sometimes had to steer visitors out of his dressing-room – they had been made speechless by his presence and all they could do was stare.)

Dinner at *La Banane* was good. The talk was about the next day's race. My French wasn't up to much; nor was the guest I was sitting next to. I glanced around the room. Nureyev was alone.

There is a basic rule for yachties: *Don't bug the guests*. The crew's job is to ensure the guests have a good time; otherwise – lay off. Same applies to any nearby VIPs in the area. I broke the rule. Got up and walked over to Rudolf Nureyev. Didn't plan it. Pure impulse.

When he was nervous, Nureyev had a curious habit of holding his wine-glass with the other hand shielding the top. He was doing this now. No doubt in his time he'd had to fend off large numbers of bores and lunatics and souvenir-hunters, so he was entitled to feel nervous. And the place was noisy; he couldn't hear what I said. He asked me to sit down. I apologized for interrupting.

'It is Mr Nureyev?'

'Yes.'

'I'm the mate on the yacht *Ocean Leopard*. We're racing around the island tomorrow. Would you care to join us?'

'Yes, I would. I enjoy sailing. I have been in Turkey.'

What he said (and what he didn't say) revealed three Nureyev characteristics: one – instant decision; two – no interest in boring details, such as what my name was or who owned the boat; three – a brisk, shorthand way with English. *I have been in Turkey*. What's that got to do with ocean racing? Later it emerged that he'd once chartered a caique and sailed with friends off the Turkish coast. That's what he meant. Obviously.

I went and told the skipper. Excellent, he said. The more the merrier. If I'd invited Mick Jagger and half the Rolling Stones, he wouldn't have been surprised; St Barts is like that. What the skipper didn't know was that he was gaining a guest but losing a mate. Although neither did I. I reckoned that ballet – in the immortal words of Alf Garnett – was soccer for poofters. A year with Nureyev taught me otherwise.

2

Strictly Professional

I picked him up in the crew car the next morning at 8.30 and got him aboard. He sat behind the mast, in the cockpit. As long as he stayed there he was safe. The boom on *Ocean Leopard* was quite high; it would miss his head. Rudolf was not tall – only shoulder-high on me. His modest height was less important than his astonishing face.

He was a Tartar, and he had the Tartar's high cheekbones, wide-set eyes and straight nose. He had a strong mouth and a neat, square chin, bracketed by lines (he was fifty-one). Once he had been beautiful; he still had an irresistible face. You couldn't not look at it. His eyes were a deep blue-grey, very alive. They made you wonder what he was going to say or do next. That was one code I never cracked.

Ocean Leopard sailed along the south coast of St Barts, and as we rounded the headland we passed his house. He'd bought it because it was close to the water, but this was the first time he'd seen it from the sea. The setting delighted him. So that was a good start. The *rosé* was flowing. Nureyev had a few glasses, chatted with people, sunbathed (he borrowed my panama hat) and watched the race. I ran the deck, nobody got hurt, nothing got broken and *Ocean*

Leopard performed well. We docked; I helped Nureyev from the boat to the quay.

'I would like to buy you dinner,' he said. 'To thank you.' That was fine by me. He said, 'Maybe on the way home we can find a place that takes American Express.' He had no cash.

We found a place. I went back to the boat, got changed, drove out to his place again. On the way to the restaurant I thought: *Here's a one-off chance to talk to Rudolf Nureyev.* What did I know? Only what I read in the papers. Russian dancer, defected, fiery temperament. I'd already met the rich and famous on boats: millionaires, statesmen, showbiz stars. I knew the drill – be polite and attentive, and don't bug the man.

Dinner was simple: he ordered a steak with no sauce, salad, we had a bottle of Montrachet between us. I asked a safe question: Did you enjoy the sail? Rudolf was enthusiastic. The trip had impressed him – not just the race but the overall competence: door-to-door transportation, no hassle. He wasn't flattering me – Rudolf never flattered anyone. It was simply that he loathed hassle.

I asked what he'd been working on. The dance jargon meant nothing to me, but he said he was soon going back to America to tour in *The King and I.* That was a musical. Nureyev didn't sound like a singer. Food came. We talked about this and that: his defection, my background. When I mentioned the benefits of my fairly normal and secure childhood, he interrupted, 'My mother said that to me. Said – money we spent on you as child. And I demanded, how much? How much I pay you back? I was six years old.' End of story. Rudolf's anecdotes were always short and sharp, and told with half a smile. It was a pleasant evening, with a lot of laughter. He called me Blue (which is my nickname) and I called him Rudolf.

I drove him home, and parked. 'Thanks very much,' I said. 'That was a really enjoyable meal.' He leaned across and poked his tongue in my ear. There was no embrace. There was no physical contact at all, except the tongue. It was unexpected and unpleasant. A strange tongue in the ear is not something I enjoy. For a moment I was lost for words. Then I said, 'I'm terribly sorry. . . .' (Why was *I* apologizing? Nothing made sense.) 'We'll be very happy to have you sailing again, but . . . but *that's not quite right.*' These last words, at least, were firm and clear.

Nureyev was not in the least troubled; in fact he was rather nonchalant. But then, he'd had a few glasses of *rosé* on the boat and half a bottle of wine at dinner; more than enough – as I later learned – to make him tipsy. 'Would you come to the house for tea in the morning?' he asked. I agreed.

As I drove back to the boat, I tried to make sense of it all. Very quickly, I knew that the tongue in the ear was the least important event of the day. Uncomfortable, and that's all. What mattered was that I had met someone unique, someone of genius. How often do you meet a genius?

Next morning I went back for tea. I made the tea. He sipped it and spat it out. '*Aaaaach!* You may not take sugar but I do!' An early lesson.

We were sitting outdoors, in the sun and out of the wind. He wore shorts and a towelling robe, with a wide-brimmed sun-hat and a shawl. He always wore a shawl, even in the sun. It was a big rectangle of tight-knit wool, with a hole for his head, so that half of it hung down his back. The front half was split; he wrapped it around his chest. Everywhere – even in the Caribbean – he worried about catching cold. He was convinced he had weak lungs.

We chatted. 'Can you move a piano?' he asked. Someone had found him a good upright in St Barts, and he had absolutely no idea how to move it. Rudolf was not mechanically minded. I got a truck, collected three or four hefty crew members, and with Rudolf directing we carried the piano up a long and steep flight of stairs. An hour later it was in his house. Rudolf was pleased: high efficiency, no hassle. Another triumph for me, Mr Organization. The loaders left. He opened a bottle of wine.

The house was dusty. It was so close to the sea that a bit of sand was inevitable, but dust was everywhere. And the kitchen sink was full of dirty pots and pans. 'Where is everybody?' I asked.

'Who?'

'Oh, you know – the maid or dresser or cook or body-guard? Anybody?'

He shrugged, which meant there was nobody; he lived alone. 'My contract with *The King and I* says I have an assistant.'

'Who's going to do it?'

'Don't know.'

We both reached the same idea at the same time. He said, 'Would you fancy it?' as I said, 'Could I do it?' That was that: for him, the decision had been made; the rest was just boring detail.

'OK,' I said. 'But this is strictly professional.' Meaning: no tongues-in-ears. He understood.

'Write your contract and show me. Leave contact numbers. Fax is very important.'

But Nureyev ended the conversation so abruptly that I came away feeling sure he'd suddenly lost all interest. It had been a bright idea that burned itself out. That sort of thing happened all the time, on yachts. Guests – the rich and famous, feeling relaxed and generous on a happy cruise – invited crew members to visit them: 'Any time you're in New York, call in, have a drink.' The form was never to take up these invitations. They were mere words. I'd heard it all a hundred times. Nureyev just made a hundred and one.

By chance, Rudolf and I met again on a yacht where he was a guest. The *Endeavour* is a stunning, sleek masterpiece, the largest single-masted yacht in the world, 130 feet long. She'd been built for Sir Thomas Sopwith in 1934 to race for the America's Cup, and recently she'd been restored (at the cost of several million dollars) by an admirable American lady, Elizabeth Meyer. The *vignerons* chartered her for a day, invited all the crews and we went sailing. It was an exhilarating experience for everyone, including Rudolf. He had a 35mm Nikon, and he shot *Endeavour* and her guests from every possible angle. Then it all turned sour.

We were sailing home. Rudolf decided to take the film out of his camera and it was empty. He blew a fuse. *Someone had stolen his film!* Huge embarrassment everywhere. Elizabeth Meyer behaved superbly. She softened Rudolf's rage: of *course*, the film must be found. There were thirty people on board. Everyone will help. Rudolf was soothed. The film was never found. The rest of us felt very uncomfortable; this man was a guest on the finest yacht afloat and he had put the owner and the charterers on the spot, all for some missing snapshots which we were convinced were more than missing: they didn't exist. The camera had never been loaded. Rudolf couldn't change a lightbulb, let alone load a camera. Now he couldn't admit his mistake, and so he had to act out a bad drama that fooled nobody. Except himself: months later, if he saw *Endeavour*, he would say, 'Ah! Some shit-person stole my film.' He was like a spoiled child among adults.

21

3

Short Intermission

After three weeks on *Ocean Leopard*, working the island chain, we reached Antigua and I was no nearer joining Nureyev on tour. In fact when I phoned New York, the people running *The King and I* did not seem desperately keen to have me on board. Disappointing, but not surprising. Out of the blue, a yacht called *Keama* arrived in Antigua. She was being delivered to Australia by a couple of old friends, Heather and Neil.

'Want to join us?' Heather said. 'We need a crew of four.'

'Who's the fourth?'

'Jane. She's flying here from Oz.' Jane was Heather's sister and a former girlfriend of mine.

That changed everything. Now I had three options. Stay on *Ocean Leopard* and be her skipper in a year. Lean on the guys in New York and take the Nureyev job. Or spend six months on *Keama*, sailing the Pacific with three good friends.

I chose *Keama*.

The other options were attractive, but not as attractive as Jane. I phoned Rudolf and told him. He said, 'Join me when you're ready.' In May 1990 *Keama* went through the Panama Canal and into the Pacific.

It's six thousand miles. We averaged six knots. You get plenty of time to think when you sail across the Pacific.

The others took a cool view of the situation. Neil pointed out, 'You've only ever had one real conversation with Nureyev, and that was pretty sketchy. It's a very loose arrangement.' This was true. 'Where's the Nureyev job going to lead?' he asked. Good question.

But what the others couldn't know was that, for me, it was time for a change. I was on a high. Life was going well and nothing was impossible. When Nureyev showed up, out of the night, the chance of working for him was irresistible. An opportunity like this was never going to happen again. The fact that he was a queen, and a prize queen at that, never bothered me. From the moment he stepped aboard *Ocean Leopard*, it was obvious to everyone – obvious from his mannerisms, his way of speaking, the way he posed for photographs and looked at the blokes in the crew. But none of this was offensive; everything had a light, amusing touch to it. Nureyev I found enormously interesting, but never intimidating. After Barnardo's it would take an awful lot to intimidate me. There was one big problem: contacting Nureyev.

Whenever we called at an island I phoned or faxed his New York agent, Andrew Grossman at Columbia Artists International. No reply. I gave up on Grossman. In Fiji I faxed Luigi Pignotti, Nureyev's agent in Milan. Amazingly, a fax came straight back, giving Rudolf's phone number on Li Galli, his island near Naples. I phoned him there, a dozen times. Nobody answered. Enough was enough: I was ready to quit. Jane had left the boat and flown ahead. She made one last call, from Sydney. Rudolf answered. He used a very deep voice when he thought people were wasting his time.

'Just send him!' he boomed A fax arrived from Luigi, listing Rudolf's American itinerary.

We delivered *Keama*. I took the opportunity to spend a few days with friends in Australia and New Zealand. By that time Rudolf was in Cleveland, Ohio. I flew via Auckland, Los Angeles and New York, with no stopovers and precious little sleep. The flight cost me a thousand dollars. I had no contract and only the briefest of verbal agreements. The plane landed at Cleveland in the afternoon of 13 October 1990: a bleak, grey, early winter's day. I took a taxi straight to the theatre. If this was a colossal mistake, at least it would be interesting. I didn't want to miss any of it.

4

Cleveland, Ohio
A Slap on the Ass

The theatre lobby was full of people, and there was a buzz of shared excitement, of keen anticipation.

These people had got there early so as to see Rudolf Nureyev arrive; and when he did, applause broke out. All this just for a matinée. It was impressive.

He saw me standing in the background. At six foot one, with blond hair, I was fairly visible, and he was expecting me. 'Ah! There you are. Good.' We went to his dressing-room. 'Where have you come from?'

'New Zealand.'

'Hmmmm.' He peered. 'Are you tired?'

'No.'

'Help me undress. Make some tea. Black, lemon, lots of sugar.' Nothing else was said until: 'Now come and watch me warm up.' He made sure the dressing-room was locked, and took me to the wings. 'Don't move.'

The curtain was down, and other dancers were already at work. When Nureyev went on stage, everyone straightened up, smiled a little, worked a bit harder. It was only a warm-up, it was only a matinée, it was only Cleveland – but Nureyev's presence turned up the current. I watched the performance from the wings, and immediately learned two things.

First, anything I got wrong was my fault. He always wanted tea. His dance ends, he comes into the wings, I pour tea. 'Too hot!' he says. 'Pour it *before* I come off!' Pointless to say I didn't know when the breaks occurred in the ballet. I should have known.

Second, dance is pain. A ballerina danced for four or five minutes, made her exit and collapsed. Something was wrong with her leg. She was in great pain: her face showed it. I took a step forward. 'Fuck off,' she said. 'Get out of my way.' She heaved herself upright. She made her entry, danced and smiled, head up. At the end of the piece she limped off to her dressing-room, still alone.

Several dancers had seen all this, and were apparently indifferent to it. I asked: What happens to her now? They were mildly surprised at the question. Oh, they said, she'll be back to dance tonight. If not, she'll lose her place. Ballet, it seemed, was an art with a streak of bloodsport in it. I'd played a lot of rugby; I knew how it felt to be kicked in the leg. In rugby you could hobble about and curse a bit; in ballet you had to look serene and dance on.

After the matinée, back to the dressing-room. Rudolf was direct but polite: Do this, do that, pack this, bring that, make sure the door is locked. Car to the hotel, Rudolf to bed, sleep until 6 p.m. Chicken soup. Car to the theatre. A crowd waiting, applauding. Warm-up, performance, dressing-room. Car to hotel, food, Rudolf to bed, sleep until late morning.

That was the routine for the next three days in Cleveland.

I fetched and carried, and waited for the boss to wake. My room was next to his. I did a lot of reading.

'We'll talk about the contract in New York,' Rudolf said. Cleveland was too busy. That meant I wasn't getting any money, but a yachtie never gets his wages when he joins a boat. You always work a month before being paid; this was no different.

Rudolf always left it dangerously late to get to the theatre for a performance. Or so it seemed. In fact he was never late; he was always just in time. He saw no point in leaving a warm hotel in order to hang around a draughty backstage. He'd spent half his life in theatres; they held no special charm for him. And even if his car got held up in traffic, he knew they couldn't start the show without him.

He was always hot; it was how he liked to be. I helped him undress, and peeled off his sweaty undershirt and hung it up to dry. When he was naked he put on his dance-strap, a sort of substantial jockstrap and the only item a ballet dancer puts on without his dresser's help. He needed assistance to get into his performance leotard, especially with the right shoulder, which had a touch of arthritis; and then into a thick wool warm-up leotard. He always wore a hat – he had dozens of woolly bobble hats. He carried five pairs of dance shoes in his bag: he'd pick out an old second-rate pair for warm-up, a favourite pair for performance.

After the warm-up he came to the wings and I helped him strip off the thick leotard. During the performance a chair and his bag were always at the ready. Whenever he came off he wanted towels (to dry himself, and to wear as a wrap if the break was long), his hat and tea. (I soon learned the breaks.) The instant the last curtain-call ended we went straight to the dressing-room: no time for gossip. Off with the dance clothes; tea; on with street clothes (no shower); back to the hotel, food, bed.

The heat was always on in his room, the windows were never opened. Same in my room. The air was dry; I woke up very thirsty. Rudolf slept in a towelling robe and a turban made of hotel towels. Under the robe he wore a double-lined sweatshirt with a big red-and-black Mickey Mouse on the front. That sweatshirt went everywhere he went – New York, St Barts, Italy, Paris, Vienna. I made sure there was always another, fresh sweatshirt on the bed. Rudolf often woke up in the night because Mickey Mouse was drenched in sweat. Not just clammy: soaking wet. The obvious thing to do was to buy a dozen Mickey Mouse sweatshirts, but Rudolf Nureyev rarely did the obvious.

Perhaps it should have been obvious that all these extreme nightsweats were abnormal. At the time, I thought they were nothing more than the inevitable consequence of always having the central heating turned up high, no windows open and too many nightclothes on. And maybe he was sweating out an illness, or keeping his muscles warm after thirty years of wear and tear. Before many months had passed, it became apparent that he was slowing down, ageing, losing weight and strength; and that was when the possibility of a link between his nightsweats and the onset of AIDS couldn't be ignored. So much fluid came out of him, he seemed to be sweating his life away. The dehydration must have had an exhausting effect, but it's fair to say that this didn't show itself in Cleveland. He sweated all night, but then he sweated all through his performances. It never seemed to slow him down.

Ballet is not often discussed by the crews of ocean-going yachts. One of the few things I knew about Rudolf Nureyev was that he and Margot Fonteyn were in the *Guinness Book of Records*. On a night in October 1964 they danced *Swan*

Lake in the Vienna Staatsoper and took eighty-nine curtain calls, a world record. In 1990 some of the old magic was still working in Cleveland. He didn't attempt any big leaps. He left the fireworks to the young dancers while he performed quiet, dramatic pieces such as 'The Overcoat' and 'The Moor's Pavanne'. Cleveland liked him.

Every day I collected great piles of programmes from people in the lobby and took them up to his room. He was in bed, with the towel-turban on his head and a big cup of soup beside him, happily signing away. He kept at it until every fan had his autograph, no matter how long it took.

Meanwhile, on-stage Rudolf stood no nonsense from anyone.

A performance ended, to loud applause. All the dancers took their bows in turn. When Rudolf took his bow, the rest of the company formed a semicircle behind him. Each time the curtain went up, they moved forward. Curtain down, they moved back. Finally, the curtain went up, and Rudolf bowed to the audience, turned, and made a small bow to the dancers, a gesture of thanks.

Some didn't bow back.

Most did, but some didn't. He's the maestro and they didn't show respect. He still had his back to the audience. His hands were clasped in front of him. As he bowed a *second* time to the dancers, he stuck his finger out, like a penis. It was lightning-quick: out and back. The audience never saw it. The dancers certainly did. They got his message: *You mess with me, I'll mess with you.* He said nothing. Next night, everyone bowed. Everyone.

Cleveland marked the end of the tour. After the last night, supporters of the ballet gave a gala reception with a buffet supper, in Nureyev's honour. There was a hell of a crowd. Everyone wanted to shake his hand, congratulate him.

31

Meanwhile I was parking the car, which wasn't easy. By the time I got upstairs he was standing alone. The buffet table, on the other hand, was very popular.

'Did you eat?' I said.

'No.' He sounded very weary. 'Nobody's given me anything, Blue.'

This was astonishing. Nureyev was their guest of honour, he'd been performing half the afternoon and all evening, and now they expected him to stand in line for food! I asked what he wanted.

'A tea first. Or fresh orange juice. I'm thirsty.'

He hadn't even been offered a drink. I barged in at the head of the buffet line, and got challenged. 'This is for the maestro,' I said. 'Give me some rice, salad, a bit of that. . . .' With food inside him, Rudolf perked up and began to circulate. I stayed close. A lady asked for his autograph and he signed her programme; then she eyed me and asked for *my* autograph. I made 'Simon Robinson' as big as 'Rudolf Nureyev', and she was delighted. (This sort of thing often happened. From then on I always signed 'Charlie Brown', which amused Rudolf.) So the evening ended pleasantly.

But it had been startling to find Rudolf standing alone and lonely, unfed and helpless. The maestro who could dominate a ballet company literally by lifting a finger was unable to help himself when left with a bunch of ordinary people. At the time I put this down to end-of-tour fatigue. But Nureyev was known as a fighter; all his life he had got what he wanted and never cared if he drew blood in the process. That reputation, it seemed, was not the whole story. At times Nureyev could be very vulnerable; even helpless. It was a surprising discovery.

After the reception, a chartered aircraft flew us to New York. It was a very small plane. We sat side by side, Rudolf with his legs stretched out. All the luggage was packed behind us. We were both too tired to talk. Somewhere over Pennsylvania he asked me to get a book out of a bag. I turned to reach behind me and he slapped me on the ass. I said nothing; just gave him the book, and looked out of the window.

No doubt he'd been slapping young men on the ass all his life, and getting away with it because he was Nureyev and they liked it. And no doubt it had often led to a damn sight more than a slap on the ass, too. Once Nureyev got the door slightly open he would feel free to walk inside. That's why our verbal agreement had been so clear-cut: ours was to be a purely professional relationship. I'd worked for only a week, and already the job was turning sour. If Nureyev couldn't keep his hands off me, it would be impossible.

We got to the Dakota at 3 a.m.

Trouble ahead.

5

The Dakota

'Fifty grand for a pair of buns'

Rudolf Nureyev had an apartment in the Dakota. Robert Tracy – his ex-boyfriend – looked after it for him. When we arrived, the first thing Robert said was, 'Lennie died yesterday.' Lennie was Leonard Bernstein. He had the next apartment.

At once Rudolf said, 'AIDS?'

Robert shook his head. Neither said any more about it. I brought the bags in. There were two striking things about the place: the great number of large oil paintings of naked men, and the stifling heat in every room. No air conditioning, no open windows. I was going to have to sweat for my living. If I stayed.

Next morning, Rudolf came into my bedroom, whistling shrilly. He demanded, 'Do you have problem with your hearing?'

'As a matter of fact, I do.' (There are some very high-pitched sounds I can't hear.)

35

He departed in disgust. What was *that* all about? Not a good start to the day. Robert cooked breakfast, which Rudolf ate (alone) in the living-room. When he'd finished I went in.

'Look, Rudolf: if last night's whack on the bum is the way it's to be, then this job's not going to work.' It was just a straight statement. It annoyed him. He scoffed, he couldn't believe I was wasting his time on something so trivial.

'We had a professional arrangement,' I said. 'I thought we'd cleared all that up.'

'Yes, yes, yes.' He made a gesture: no more talk. But that wasn't going to solve the problem.

'You don't touch me,' I insisted. 'I'm not your boyfriend.' I was standing between Rudolf and the door. One rule I learned in childcare was: in a confrontation, never block the other person's exit, or he'll feel trapped and maybe become violent.

Rudolf became violent. His self-control dissolved and he punched me in the stomach and stormed out of the room.

It was a good punch. Rugby players grow up believing that ballet dancers are wimps. Try lifting a woman above your head, without twitching, and then letting her down as lightly as a feather, time after time. Rudolf had been doing that and much more for over thirty years. He had biceps like a middleweight. I wasn't hurt but I was winded. I stared at the wall. *Bloody hell*, I thought. Then I got on with some work.

Later that day Robert told me that Rudolf had gone to him and said, 'Blue has no sense of humour.'

'Well . . . Blue's very straight, Rudolf.' (Robert placed me as soon as he saw me; he knew I was not in competition for Rudolf's affections.) 'Blue doesn't really enjoy that stuff.'

Rudolf brooded. 'Maybe I shouldn't have. . . .' He shrugged his shoulders.

Next time we met up, he said, ' I'm sorry, but you must not make me do things like that.' He wasn't heavy-handed; he was quiet and amicable. I never challenged him again. It was a very long time before he laid hands on me again, and by then my job had very little future.

Robert also told me what the boss had meant when he asked about my hearing. Whenever Rudolf wanted me, he didn't call, he whistled between his teeth. This whistle came from ballet. If he was rehearsing the company, and he wanted to stop the dancers or the orchestra (or both), he knew that shouting or stamping didn't always work, but a high-pitched, penetrating whistle did.

It was the first sound he made whenever he woke. I learned to be awake before him: a whistle would soon be on its way. His habit of whistling for me shocked some people. It never bothered me. Rudolf had his system, and it worked.

It's called the Dakota because when it was built, in the last century, New Yorkers said it was so far uptown you might as well go and live in Dakota.

Now it's on Central Park West at 72nd Street: a hulking great apartment building of dark red sandstone, dotted with gargoyles. It's no longer remote but it is unique and, in a sense, isolated. For a long time it has been occupied by writers and artists and musicians, who have turned it into a cultural colony in the middle of Manhattan. John Lennon lived and died there. Rudolf had a big, spacious apartment on the second level.

We stayed at the Dakota for a week. He slept a lot. He had been working more or less continuously for the past eighteen months, first on a six-month tour of America playing the lead in *The King and I*, and then dancing with various ballet companies (Cuba, Naples), before the American

37

tour of *Nureyev and Friends.* Much of the day he was in bed. Much of the night he was on the phone, gossiping, catching up on news in the dance world. Rudolf was a phone person. He liked its immediacy; writing would have taken too long, always assuming he *could* write. I don't think he could, certainly not in English. In this respect Rudolf was semi-illiterate.

He could read English, and he enjoyed reading – he liked the London *Sunday Times* and the *International Herald Tribune,* and he was deep in Bertrand Russell's *History of Western Philosophy* – but I never knew him to write anything. If there was no alternative and a letter (more probably a fax) must be sent, he dictated something and I straightened out his scrambled English. Similarly it was pointless to write to Rudolf. The last time he danced with the Royal Ballet in London, the head stage-door keeper used to hand him his mail when he arrived; Rudolf always threw it on the floor. (When Rudolf left, the same man used to throw the same bundle of letters in front of him and say, 'Now you pick them up, Rudi!' – but of course he never did.) The only time I knew Rudolf to read a letter was when it came from his agent – and then it had to be very urgent.

His New York agent was Andrew Grossman. He called on Rudolf a couple of times and buttered him up like a Channel swimmer: *maestro, maestro, maestro.* . . . Rudolf had heard it all before. Still, he listened; Grossman's agency, Columbia Artists International, had done much to keep him in work; they'd made him a lot of money. Grossman was a typically tough, efficient New York agent, very focused on getting big fees for big clients. I never saw him eat anything but steak or spaghetti. At one dinner party there was neither, and he ate nothing.

Grossman must have seen Nureyev's boyfriends come and go, and he probably thought I was the latest in a long line. Anyway, he ignored me. Many people treated me in a distant or formal manner, for the very good reason that they were afraid of Rudolf, or in awe of him, and they didn't want him to suspect that they were trying to poach his property. So nobody made a pass at me. This made my life easier. It was also a measure of Nureyev's power.

Money was always a problem. Not money for the big items, like air fares or the rent at the Dakota. Money for the house-keeping, petty cash to buy odds and sods – *that* money was a problem. Yet Nureyev was rich. Later I did some of his banking in New York – depositing cash or cheques, trans-ferring funds – and what I handled was just a tiny fraction of his wealth. The problem was getting him to hand over enough of it to buy groceries. There were millions of dollars' worth of art hanging on the walls. The housekeep-ing was on a shoestring.

Robert Tracy and I did the shopping. Rudolf gave us money, but he had almost no idea of how much anything cost. He'd fish out a hundred dollar bill, which would buy a lot of pasta and salad, but he expected a few bottles of very good wine, too; and good Montrachet or Pouilly-Fuisse made a big hole in a hundred bucks. It was no good asking him for more cash; we just had to make it stretch. Robert showed me where to shop, what to buy; he was helpful. We were never the warmest of friends. His world wasn't my world.

He'd had rotten luck. About ten years before I met him, Rudolf had spotted him in the *corps de ballet*, pulled him out, promoted his talent (which was considerable) and danced with him. Robert was then in his early twenties. For a while they were lovers, but Robert soon became afraid of the risks that were inseparable from Rudolf's hectic promis-cuity, and he left him. They were reunited but not as lovers.

They lived together as good friends. Robert tried to warn Rudolf of the dangers of his sexual lifestyle. Rudolf never changed; still, they were a fairly happy couple until one night – it must have been about 1988 – when they were staying at Rudolf's farmhouse in Virginia. Robert took the car and went to get a video. What exactly happened, he never knew. He woke up in hospital three days later. The car was a write-off and his legs were smashed.

It was a horrible irony that Robert, who had tried to persuade Rudolf to lead a safer life, should be the one who could never dance again. After huge amounts of physiotherapy he could walk but – as he told me – he wasn't going anywhere. He seemed uptight, unhappy, lonely and older than thirty-something. His future looked bleak. I asked him if he played an instrument. 'My body,' he said. End of conversation. He was trying to write a book on Nureyev, and he wrote pieces for dance magazines; they kept getting chopped to the bone. Robert was not a great writer, but he had to do something.

For he had no money of his own. People thought it was wonderful, living in the Dakota. They didn't realize he was broke. Nureyev let him live there rent-free and expected him to look after the place, so Nureyev got an unpaid caretaker. This meant that Robert had to get people in to solve maintenance problems, or make alterations, or do repairs. 'What do I know about building repairs?' he said to me. 'I want to get on with my book.' One day, walking along 72nd Street, we met a beggar on the sidewalk. Robert gave him some change, and as we walked on he said, 'What am I doing? I haven't any money! *I* should be begging!' He shook his head and laughed, but it wasn't a funny joke.

The bitter truth was that, although Robert retained some affection for Rudolf, very little (if any) of that affection was returned. Robert found himself almost a servant in the house of a former lover. If there was a chore to be done, 'Oh, Robert can do that,' Rudolf said; often it was 'that shit-boy Robert', and Robert got neither thanks nor money for doing the chore. Nureyev was not a generous man. He treated Robert little better than any other damaged dancer: if he couldn't perform he was worthless. Of course Rudolf applied the same ruthless standards to himself. It was this unswerving determination that had taken him to the top of his world and kept him there for the best part of thirty years. In a dancer it was admirable. Perhaps Rudolf could never afford to be anything but a dancer.

What Rudolf liked about the Dakota was the space. You walked in through tall doors and the first thing you saw was a colossal church organ, complete with pipes. He was always talking about making it work; thank God it didn't. A long corridor was lined with classical paintings of male nudes. Wherever you went there were wide hallways, high ceilings, large rooms. He could relax in the Dakota.

At the back, next to the kitchen, was the bedroom that Robert and I shared. I had a Queen Anne bed – too short for me, and therefore not comfortable – and one wall was entirely covered by a vast medieval city map, unframed. It was an original, not a copy, and extremely valuable. It always worried me that the relentless heat might damage the parchment.

Rudolf lavished money on furniture and fabrics. He had a four-poster in his bedroom, and a harpsichord (which he played) made in 1725. I damn near unmade it in 1990. I was replacing lightbulbs when the rickety old stepladder, property of the Dakota, swayed wildly towards the harpsichord. I stuck out a hand and grabbed the curtains just in time. How much would a 1725 harpsichord set you back nowadays? I broke out in a cold sweat, on top of my normal hot sweat.

The best room in the apartment was the living-room, overlooking Central Park. It was big enough to be a gallery. Rudolf hung some truly heroic pictures on the living-room walls: two of the oil paintings were at least nine feet by six feet, and there were many others, all eighteenth-century classical stuff. His taste was easily defined. He liked male nudes: there were square yards of muscular men, all naked except for a helmet or perhaps a scabbard, and usually engaged in mortal combat with a lion or with other equally naked and muscular men. He had paid a lot of money for this art, and when it came up for auction after his death it fetched high prices, so he had a good eye. Personally, I found it all a bit repetitive, but it was his living-room and his art, and he revelled in it.

Especially the statue. Rudolf had recently bought an ancient Greek statue for $50,000. It was a torso: no head, arms or legs. The figure was powerful, although there were pouches of surplus flesh just above the hips: an honest Greek sculptor. Rudolf liked the buttocks. The living-room had two long, comfortable sofas that he could plop into. More than once he whistled for me: 'Move the bum.' I'd get Robert to help, and we'd rotate the statue a few degrees. Rudolf would be at the other side of the room. 'Bit more.' We'd give it another nudge. 'Ah. That's what I like.' He'd got a perfect view of the bum. And why not? If you're going to pay fifty grand for a pair of buns, you might as well see them at their best.

Rudolf himself was often naked in the apartment, but not for show. In a working life that demanded he wear strange and restrictive costumes, he liked the freedom of wearing nothing. It made no difference to Robert or to me. Robert had seen it all before, and I'd seen more than enough naked men in rugby club dressing-rooms and on yachts. Rudolf reckoned that he'd had the perfect physique for a dancer. (He wasn't boasting; he just said what he thought.) His neck was powerful. His shoulders were broad for his height. He always complained of weak lungs, but his chest was big and strong and he had biceps to match. His legs were extremely muscular, especially the thighs. It was this superb combination – legs, torso, neck, arms – that enabled him to go on lifting ballerinas long after most dancers gave up. The trick of a faultless lift, he said, was speed: quick up, quick down, with no tremors, no rush, no thump. He made it look easy.

But although he kept his body in good working order, he was no Greek god. He was fifty-two by now, and it showed. Time spares nobody, not even Nureyev. Apart from his amazing face, there was nothing to make you look twice.

One day an attractive woman from *The New York Times* arrived; Rudolf had promised an interview. I showed her into the living-room and before I could tell him she'd arrived, his voice boomed, 'Blue, where did you put. . . .' and he strode in, stark naked.

'Ah, Rudolf, this is. . . .'

'Ooooh!' he said. The sound came out like a cork from a bottle. It was one of the very few occasions when I saw him embarrassed. He went red in the face, covered himself, and backed out.

She just smiled. It was, after all, the Dakota.

It's difficult to work for someone who makes the rules but can't explain them. Nureyev was the greatest name in ballet; he was the standard against which any other male ballet star – men like Baryshnikov and Mukhamedov – were measured. He had no patience with anyone who didn't instinctively and immediately understand what he wanted. I remember watching him rehearse Evelyn

Desutter. 'You have to. . . .' he said, and flicked his wrist. '*Potage*.' She nodded. Later I worked it out: stir the soup, rotate like a spoon in the soup. When he gave orders in the Dakota, he could be just as cryptic. Directions to an office or house might be, 'Go over hill. Red roof.' It was useless asking for more information: Rudolf knew where the place was, and so should I. He spoke a language of his own, very abbreviated, often oblique, and if I couldn't learn it that was my tough luck, because he certainly wasn't going to adjust to *me*. There were times when I was utterly bewildered.

Once I said to Robert Tracy, 'What do I do?'

'I can't tell you. You'll find a way. *Your* way.'

Robert knew Rudolf better than anyone, and he knew there was no magic formula for satisfying him. I asked Robert what was the best time of day to speak to Rudolf. 'I used to talk to him when we were in bed together, last thing at night,' he said. 'Of course, that doesn't help you, Blue.'

So I stumbled on, working by trial and error and occasionally by blind instinct. Once I happened to be in the living-room while he was on the mobile phone. Whoever it was, they wouldn't agree to what he wanted or they talked too much. He hated that. Suddenly his rage boiled over and he hurled the phone at the wall, just missing an oil painting that had cost him a quarter of a million dollars. Luck or judgement? Who knows? I put my hand on his shoulder and said, 'Can I do anything?' He slumped, and all the rage drained out.

'No, it's all right,' he said. And off he toddled. Rudolf's fury was straight up and straight down. Once you knew that, handling it was simple. Not easy, but simple.

Leonard Bernstein's death upset Rudolf, as much as he allowed the death of any friend to upset him, which was not a lot: he grieved briefly and then got on with life. But the loss cast a gloom over our week in New York, because Nureyev and Bernstein had been neighbours as well as friends. Between Lenny's studio, where he had two magnificent concert grands, and Rudolf's bedroom, there was a party wall.

'I used to tap on wall at night,' Rudolf said. 'Send message in code to Lenny.' He demonstrated: *Boing!* 'Hello, Lenny!' *Boing-boing-boing!* 'Hello, Rudi!'

If it's not true, it deserves to be true.

On our last day in New York there was to be a memorial service in Leonard's apartment. The Dakota was completely surrounded by police: police cars, police motorbikes, cops on every rooftop that might hold a sniper. It wasn't so long since John Lennon had been murdered as he left the Dakota. Now big names were turning up from all parts to say farewell to Leonard Bernstein, and the NYPD was taking no chances. It was easy for Rudolf to go next door. But the timing was awkward – we had to catch a flight to Milan – and he said, 'I don't like these things. They upset me.' He agonized up to the last minute. 'Oh, we'll go. I'll say a few words.'

He did, and explained about his Milan flight, and we rushed down the stairs.

That made us the first out of the service. The media – there were TV crews everywhere – closed in. The limo was waiting. I shoved people out of the way, made sure Rudolf got in safely. As I followed him, a press photographer barged forward and shouted, 'What d'you think of Leonard Bernstein's death, Mr Baryshnikov?'

The limo accelerated away. Rudolf looked at me. 'What did he say?' he asked. He hadn't heard. I told him, and he laughed for a block and a half. 'Wrong again!' he said, with boyish glee. 'They got it wrong again.'

6

La Scala
The *Nutcracker* Olympics

Milan had elegance. Milan had respect. Rudolf liked that.

When he arrived at the Cleveland theatre, a stagehand would say, 'Hi, buddy.' When he walked into La Scala, the man sweeping the stage wore a well-cut suit and a good tie. He tucked the broom under his arm and shook Rudolf's hand. 'Maestro! How are you? I much enjoyed your last performance.'

At La Scala, even if all you do is sweep the stage, you're proud of it. There is never any panic or hassle at La Scala. Always respect, always 'maestro'. Rudolf enjoyed respect; he'd earned it.

We were met by Robert de Warren, the ballet master. 'Ah, Rudolf! How nice to have you back.' At that time there was a fad for motorists to have toy dogs that nodded inside their rear windows. Rudolf called de Warren 'the nodding dog'. 'Did you have a good flight?' de Warren asked.

'Yes, yes.' Rudolf wanted to get on.

De Warren looked at me. 'Ah . . . and who are you? I don't think we've met before. It's always nice to. . . .'

'Robert, this Blue.' Now Rudolf was really impatient.

'And are you . . . dancing? Or possibly involved in. . . .'

Rudolf cut in with a voice like an axe. 'This – Blue. He knows *nothing*. He is completely . . .' Rudolf's hand swept straight down in front of his face, signalling total ignorance. De Warren blinked a bit, but he got the message: I was Rudolf's gofer and nothing else. If people thought I was part of the production they might try to use me as leverage on the maestro; it had happened before. Now everyone knew the score. Good. He got to work.

We were staying in a hotel in Milan; a very good hotel. On the second morning, Rudolf said, 'Run me a bath at 3.15.'

'OK, good. I'll do that, Rudolf.'

He stared. I smiled and nodded; I knew what he wanted. He didn't seem reassured. '*Well?*' he demanded. I thought hard. Well what? But rage was starting to show in his eyes. 'The *bath!*' he shouted.

'Yes, 3.15. I'll run it when. . . .'

'No, no! Not this afternoon! *Bath knobs!* Set bath knobs at angle of 3.15! *Now!*'

'Now?'

'*Now! Eediott!*'

Rudolf knew this hotel well. He remembered that if you set the bath taps at the position of 3.15, the water was at just the right temperature – in his case, very hot. So, for me, another code was broken. And his fury evaporated like the steam from the bath.

Next day he told me not to make the tea any more. 'Your tea is . . . uninspiring. Let Luigi make it.'

I'm English; I'm supposed to know how to make tea. Wherever we went I carried teabags; my clothes smelt of Earl Grey. But my brew didn't inspire the boss. I watched Luigi. Rudolf liked lemon, and I'd been dunking a big chunk of lemon. Luigi – formerly his masseur and now his agent – cut a lemon in half and got his powerful fist around it and squeezed. So now I knew. Later, when Rudolf said, 'Shoehorn', I found out what it was in Italian – *calzante* – and got one fast. Dance shoes are tight. He'd lost his *calzante*. No *calzante*, no practice. I was learning.

He was in Milan not to dance, but to direct *The Nutcracker*, the traditional Christmas-season ballet. For a week and a half he and I sat on the stage, facing the company, and he created his vision of *Nutcracker*, piece by piece, act by act. He never relaxed, and never let the company relax. For a week and a half he drilled them. He made them sweat. It was a great test of strength. Could he inspire the company? He had only ten days of rehearsal, and just to intensify the pressure, two *other* productions of *Nutcracker* would open in Milan on the same night as his. To succeed, Nureyev had to win gold in this bizarre Olympiad.

Here was Rudolf at his best. He was dedicated to dance, totally focused on dance, dance was his reason for existence. When he saw great talent, he encouraged it. He didn't give a damn what others thought; he knocked down any obstacles in order to give that talent its chance. He told me how, at the Palais Garnier in Paris, in the winter of 1984–5, he had seen a nineteen-year-old dancer in *Swan Lake*, and said, 'That girl's brilliant – much better than the prima ballerina.' Not everyone agreed. Rudolf publicly promoted Sylvie Guillem, and she *was* brilliant. She went to the top. There were others: Evelyn Desutter, Bryony Brind, Charles Jude. He never stopped looking. Rehearsal had ended for the day. We were on stage at La Scala, he was making sure I had the bag, the scarf. . . . 'Flask?' he said. 'OK.' Then he stopped.

The stage was still full of dancers, waiting for the

maestro to leave. He was looking at a boy. All male dancers are called boys, but this really was a boy.

'Hmmm. Get the boy's name. He may be good for *Death in Venice*.' (Which Rudolf was due to direct and dance in, at Verona.) Dance was Nureyev's life. And the boy? It turned out he wasn't good enough to dance in *Death in Venice*. Too bad. Next!

For Nureyev, people were divided into two sorts. He described one sort as 'He bin good to me', and the other sort as 'He bin mean to me'. Luigi Pignotti fell into both categories, sometimes on the same day. This was unfair, for Luigi was one of the best friends Rudolf had; but who ever said that Rudolf had to be fair to anyone?

Luigi had been Rudolf's personal masseur. That was all he did; he travelled around the world and pounded and pummelled the maestro's muscles so he could go on stage and get the last ounce of strength out of them. Luigi was an extremely powerful man. He needed to be.

Then Rudolf began steering bits of work Luigi's way – small dance shows, modest companies – and gradually Luigi became a minor impresario. When Rudolf danced in Italy, it was a Pignotti production. In time Luigi became a major impresario, putting together shows as far away as Japan, high-quality shows. And now he was Rudolf's agent in Europe. So they were very close – which didn't stop Rudolf taking every opportunity to remind Luigi (and anyone else listening) that he was just a masseur whom Rudolf had groomed into a successful businessman.

And Rudolf made a lot of demands, some great, some petty, some impossible. When Luigi couldn't deliver, Rudolf decided that *he bin mean to me* and there would be an immediate divorce. That was Rudolf's word for it. Luigi soldiered on. When Rudolf needed him again – next week?

next day? – the divorce was forgotten.

In 1990 Luigi was in his forties, a big, strong, cheerful bloke, very warm-hearted, very Italian. He was glad to see me. Rudolf treated Luigi rather like Robert Tracy; just picked up the phone and told him to do this, or get that: bits of shopping, small chores. The calls never stopped, and Luigi had an international business to run. Now he could answer: *'Rudolf, you've got Blue to do this.'*

As soon as Rudolf wasn't around, Luigi said to me, 'Always remember: this man is an absolute individual. Never judge him by anything or anyone you have known before. Start afresh. He is absolutely unique.'

Two days before opening night, he fired one of the principal girl dancers.

It was midday. Rehearsals had gone well. Rudolf said, 'Fine, good. Lunch.' As he got up from his chair, this girl walked forward and said, 'May I have a word, maestro?' There was no obvious problem, and most people were only too glad to get off-stage for the lunch break. *Hello,* I thought. *Something's up.*

'Yes,' Rudolf said.

'I would like my boyfriend to be the principal dancer in this *Nutcracker*, because I think he can dance well with me.'

'Ah. . . .' By now we were all moving towards the wings. 'I don't think so. The one I selected is going to do it.'

'Well, if my boyfriend doesn't do it, *I* won't do it.'

Rudolf, still walking, turned to Robert de Warren. 'Find another girl for opening night.'

'Ah!' she said. 'What I *meant* was . . . I mean of course I'll dance opening night.'

Rudolf gave her a short stare. 'You sure?'

'Yes, I'll dance . . . I just wondered if you'd really . . . thought . . . about. . . .'

'Yes, I'd thought.' To Robert de Warren, 'You don't need to find another girl for opening night. Lunch.'

Fired and re-hired, all in twenty seconds. It wasn't clever to threaten Nureyev with an ultimatum. Maestro means master, and he was just that. He paid a small price for this dominance: nobody would sit at his table in La Scala's canteen. The dancers were too in awe of him. They admired him beyond measure, but he lived in a different world; or so they thought. He didn't enjoy this isolation, and sometimes he'd beckon to someone, 'Come and sit.' But usually Robert and I were his only companions at lunch.

On opening night he sat in the wings. He wasn't wearing tails or black tie; he was in smart-casual: white shirt, dark trousers, black shoes. A tie would have been nice, too. 'Phone Luigi. Tell him, get me blue tie.' (Habits die hard.)

'There's a blue tie in my bag.'

'Yes? I'll wear that.'

Rudolf didn't know how to knot a tie; he'd always been a polo-neck sweater man. I stood behind him and tied his tie. This didn't embarrass him: all his life people had been dressing him, tacking bits on here, fixing buttons there.

The performance was a stunning success. The emotional charge built up and up as the evening wore on. At the end there was a storm of applause, a glorious release of delight into noise. The dancers took curtain after curtain and the audience was roaring for Nureyev. The dancers came to him, but he wouldn't leave the wings. 'No. It's not my work,' he said. 'You're the dancers. You did the work.'

The audience didn't hear that, and it would have made no difference if they had: they knew better, they wanted Nureyev. The applause was so hungry it was irresistible, and in the end he had to appear. There was a single, vast roar. Flowers came flying onto the stage. The warmth of affection was overwhelming. Backstage there was a great surge of pride in everyone, pride in being part of Rudolf Nureyev's creation. He said, 'Thank you very much.' He stepped back. His was a very brief curtain call: a true finale to the evening. The applause died. The show was over.

The dancers, still sweating, formed a big semicircle around him. As we walked away I congratulated him.

'Did you like that?'

'Wonderful. Brilliant.'

'Yes, I always liked that one. That was a good one.' Very calm, almost offhand, as if to say: *The kids done good.* But the truth was obvious – after thirty years in the business, he still got a special kick out of that last curtain call, even if it lasted only a few seconds. 'Let's get some dinner,' he said.

First, however, we drove to the other two *Nutcracker* productions – not to see the show but to check the audience. The first place was three-quarters full, the second only half full. That made dinner even better.

He kept the tie.

7

Paris

'You shout, I won't cry'

In Paris we finally got around to the contract. A lawyer friend had advised me, 'Make it bold. Make it clear.' So Clause 1 said:

I am your personal assistant.
I am not your boyfriend.

This had nothing to do with AIDS. At that time nobody had told me that Nureyev had AIDS – nobody ever did, in fact – and he certainly didn't look ill. In any case, even if I had known that he had AIDS I would still have worked for him. At Barnardo's in London I'd been planning to take a job in a residential centre for HIV-infected adolescents; the disease held no terrors for me. Clause 1 was worded because Nureyev had made a pass at me. The wording would have been the same if I'd been working for a ballerina who fancied me as her boyfriend. I wanted to eliminate all confusion about who did what, and why.

The contract was short. It listed my duties: drive, carry bags, handle communications, look after property maintenance, make flight reservations, take care of laundry, cleaning and clothes, in fact do everything except cook. I couldn't cook. Salary: US$1,500 a month. (On *Ocean Leopard* I got $1,200 a month.)

Rudolf said, 'OK, Yes. I very much like this *relationship* part. Important there is no personal relationship. People get upset when I speak my feelings. If I shout, you must not get upset.'

'No problem.'

'People tried to help and when they asked, "How is dinner?" and I said "It's shit", they go away and cry. Drama.'

'You shout, I won't cry.'

'Good. There may be some massage, we'll talk about this. You have to cook.'

I protested, 'I'm not a cook.'

'It's impossible. You cannot be stern. We go to isolated places. One have to learn.' He read the rest. 'Girlfriends . . . Girls . . . It's impossible for you to have girlfriends while you are with me.'

This was a blow. Not unexpected, but still a blow.

'Not possible to bring them back to the house,' he explained. 'For a cup of tea, or . . . too embarrassing. Too much for me to have to stand and greet.' No passion, no self-pity. He was rather stoical. So was I. I was so bloody stoical it hurt. But already we'd lived in four cities in five weeks. At this rate I'd never have a girlfriend, so I might as well learn to cook.

Later Rudolf said, 'I was wondering.' Whenever I heard that, I braced myself. Anything might follow. He might say *Can I borrow your hat?* or *Should we buy some dynamite?* 'This salary,' he said. 'It's fifteen hundred . . . what is that, Blue?'

'American dollars, Rudolf.' Currencies confused him.

'I was wondering. If I paid for your flight from New Zealand, can I pay you a thousand dollars a month?'

If I worked for Rudolf for a year, I'd lose five thousand dollars. But would I last a year? I agreed to his offer. Now, looking back, I know that it wasn't even an offer. When he said *I was wondering*, he had already decided. Either I agreed or I quit.

Nureyev owned six homes, on three continents, and he was thinking of adding a seventh. There was a Nureyev Foundation. He could have stocked a couple of art galleries with his paintings. Why did saving five hundred dollars a month matter so much? God knows I wasn't overpaid, considering I was on duty seven days a week, from the moment he woke until he went to bed. There was certainly a streak of the haggling, penny-pinching peasant in him, but there was something else, too. Nureyev had worked for everything he owned. He had literally sweated for it all. He had a lot of money and he was happy to spend it: $50,000 for the statue in the Dakota was a small example. That didn't make him careless of its value. Nobody had ever given him money. Why should I be treated differently? If I wanted more, I'd have to sweat for it.

I altered the contract and made two copies. 'There's a space for both of us to sign.'

'I don't sign anything.' And he didn't. Autographs by the thousand but never a document, if he could avoid it. 'If you're not happy – go. If I don't want you, you'll go.'

As I put the copies away, he turned and said, 'I suppose the buggery's still out, is it?'

'Absolutely.'

We both laughed. Nureyev couldn't tolerate long, serious talk. When discussion grew heavy, something outrageous popped out. He couldn't resist it.

We spent a week in Paris: a thoroughly cock-eyed week, a week of plans made and scrapped, of sudden decisions, of futile attempts by me to second-guess what Nureyev was up to; and all carried out in such dazzlingly splendid décor that it made the Dakota look drab.

Rudolf was a great collector. He spent many millions, in many countries, and most of the stuff ended up in Paris. The place had a special meaning for him. This was where he had defected in 1961, a skinny kid with a few francs, a cheap suitcase and a raging talent. Many years later he came back as artistic director of the Paris Opéra Ballet. He knew his way around Paris. He had hired one of the greatest designers in the world, Emilio Carcano, to turn his art collection into a home. I thought it looked more like a stage-set than a home; but then, Rudolf was more at home on a stage than anywhere else.

The biggest room – known as the salon – was (he told me) inspired by a room in one of the royal Spanish residences. The walls were covered with panels of Cordoba leather which Nureyev himself had found in Spain. These panels were three hundred years old and so wonderfully decorated as to be works of art in themselves, but they were half-hidden by his collection of French paintings, dating back to the fourteenth century. Huge brass chandeliers (eighteenth-century Polish) carried scores of candles. And all that was just the start, just a hint of the overwhelming splendour. It overwhelmed me. There was no escape. Look away from the hand-painted harpsichord and you saw a swathe of rare kimonos hanging like curtains. Look away from the kimonos and you saw sofas covered in velour so rich it glowed.

So much for the salon. Moving now into the dining-room – never mind. Just take my word for it. And to look after the place: nobody. Nureyev had no staff. His nephew lived in the next apartment; Rudolf always called him 'that shit-boy'. His niece was in the apartment above; she was 'the witch upstairs'. He also had a sister in France, living in his house in Monte Carlo; he had no words for her. Rudolf had brought all three of them out of Russia, which couldn't have been easy and must have been expensive. From what I could see, he got precious little thanks. 'And everybody was unhappy,' he said to me, drily, 'and they thought they should get more.'

Rudolf had no staff, but Douce François, a middle-aged lady, came in from time to time to check the place was OK and to stack the mail. She was one of several long-time and long-suffering female admirers dotted around the world who had given their hearts to Rudolf for twenty years or more. Rudolf gave them little or nothing in return. Douce adored him; years ago she had wanted to have his child, which was not Rudolf's idea of fun. It was Douce who had burst into tears when he was candid about her cooking.

Rudolf told me to take care of the mail. There was a huge pile of it. I didn't know where to start.

'You will overcome,' he said, a favourite remark. He was right. I binned the junk, filed the stuff he needed and sent the rest to Luigi Pignotti. Rudolf's job was dance. My job was to clear the decks so that he could do his job. That much was clear. Everything else was confusion.

Each day was a mystery because Rudolf either never told me what he was going to do, or told me and then changed his mind and didn't say so. He made plans and scrapped them, all day, all week, and blamed me for not being ready. One night he announced, 'Right. Now we have to go. Get a taxi.' Where? 'Paris Opéra.' He was surprised that I was surprised.

I phoned for a taxi. Ten minutes, they said.

One minute later, 'Where's the taxi? Is it now?' Suddenly

it was frantically urgent. 'Go down!' he shouted. 'Get a taxi!'

I dashed downstairs and ran to the corner, waving furiously. No taxi stopped. But meanwhile, the taxi I ordered had arrived, and Rudolf and the shit-boy nephew were in it, and Rudolf was steaming because now he was late and it was all my fault. 'Where are you?' he roared. I ran back. 'Get in the damn car! Eediott!'

'I'm sorry. I was trying to flag a taxi down.'

'*Flag a taxi down?*' This simple explanation utterly infuriated him. 'You're standing there looking like a *tomato*.' It was amazing how much vitriol he packed into that *tomato*.

We got there late, but so what? Everyone else was late too. Rudolf missed nothing. He just wanted to arrive when he wanted to arrive. On such occasions Rudolf had zero patience. He had promised himself a treat and he must have it *now*.

Every night we went to an opera or ballet, or to a dinner party; sometimes both. Every day I worked, cleaning, shopping, running around, sweating. The apartment was as relentlessly hot as the Dakota. I was fit but the routine was exhausting. One night Rudolf announced that the Paris Opéra was holding a gala performance. 'You must come,' he ordered. 'To see this dancer. We go to Paris Opéra.'

I'd been sweating for twelve hours. I was knackered. 'I'd rather stay and cook dinner, Rudolf.'

Scorn made his voice loud and deep. '*Fuuuuuck* dinner. You always overcook anyway.'

He was right. It was a brilliant evening. We came out at 11.30. Rudolf was with some friends; the group was one too many for a taxi. I said I'd walk back. 'OK,' Rudolf said. They vanished into the night.

I got home at midnight. As I walked in, six of them were sitting around, having drinks. 'Right!' he said. 'Dinner!' I cooked dinner for seven. We ate at one in the morning. I couldn't complain: it was all in the contract, and I wrote the contract.

Dance is drama, and drama is conflict. Nureyev liked a little drama in everything. If he couldn't find it, he made it – even in signing autographs.

Wherever we went, people came up to him with things to sign, often photographs. 'Certainly,' he'd say, and do it. As they walked away they always looked at his autograph. When they'd got so far, he'd call out, 'Excuse me!' and hold up the pen. They'd apologize, and he'd give them their pen and a big smile too. So he'd spiced up the chore with a little flash of drama.

But sometimes that flash could leave scorch-marks. The person would give him both the pen and the photograph. Rudolf would sign, and then hold them out – pen in one hand, photograph in the other. And if the person reached for the pen *first*, Rudolf moved it away. Not far. Just out of reach. If they stretched, he moved it a bit further. Then he'd say, 'What d'you want? This shit pen? Or this other thing, that you came for?'

They were usually defensive: 'Ah, but I just—'

'Cheap, crappy Bic,' he'd say. He wasn't out to humiliate. He just wanted to make a point. We called it the 'pen move'. Sometimes Rudolf would do it on a person so thick that he (or she) didn't know what was happening. As we walked on, I'd say, 'Nice pen move there, Rudolf.'

He'd say, 'You saw that? Yesss. Piz*daaat*.' Which is a very dirty word in Russian.

Everyone wanted something from Nureyev. This had been going on for thirty years. He was entitled to get a little something back. All in all, Rudolf seemed to be in good form in Paris, full of fizz, the cheers of La Scala still fresh in his memory. Or so it seemed. Nureyev was a much more complex individual than that.

Perhaps the pills should have been a clue. They came in a packet of fifteen sheets, each containing rows of capsules that could be punched out of the foil backing. Rudolf always kept one sheet; he gave me the rest to carry. The capsules were blue and white, with nothing to identify them – no marking, no label. He didn't say what they were for and I didn't ask. They might have been anti-allergy drugs, or something to relieve his arthritis, or treatment for any one of a hundred other ailments. I didn't pay them much attention. Neither did Rudolf: often he forgot to take them.

One thing was definite. From Paris we were going to Cuba.

On the final day I tidied the apartment, dumped the milk, packed the bags and went out and picked up the airline tickets from our travel agent. Destination: St Barts. What had happened to Cuba? God knows. Rudolf had phoned Milan and told Luigi to organize these tickets. Why use Luigi? God knows that, too. It might have been just a whim. Why hadn't he told me? Why should he? Wherever it was, I was going there with him.

But Rudolf seemed strangely reluctant to leave the apartment. In the taxi to the airport he was not a happy man. In the terminal he stood and looked around.

'Oh,' he said, glumly, 'I don't want to fly today. Too tired.'

Back to the apartment. I unpacked, bought food. He slept. Next day we flew to St Barts. That is, we left Paris for St Barts. Unfortunately there were delays, and we missed our connecting flight, and it all turned into a shambles. He should have travelled the day before; then he wouldn't have found himself on a small boat, throwing up into the choppy Caribbean at midnight. I was all right. I liked the Caribbean.

Rudolf is hot and irritated after a performance during the British tour – but nothing will stop him signing every last autograph. No pens here. One large felt-tip marker and a flick of the wrist. 'Next!'

A tribute to the maestro: dancers thank Nureyev after the last night of the British tour. He is beginning to look a bit drained and shrunken, but he's still alert enough to stand in front of some colour

Below: Rudolf after the final performance of the British tour, in Brighton, 18 May 1991. The smile is genuine – the tour is over and he's safe with friends. *Second from left:* Maude Gosling, his mentor for nearly thirty years. *Far right:* the designer, Tessa Kennedy. *Far Left:* Blue Robinson

Approaching the airstrip at St Barts offered a nice choice between overshooting into the sea or clipping the traffic on the hill road. I saw two planes end up in the surf. Rudolf hated flying in or out, but then he hated flying anywhere

Rudolf's place on St Barts was just a beach-front house. He had it extended – without planning permission, of course. Its remoteness satisfied him, and he enjoyed the sound of spray hitting the roof

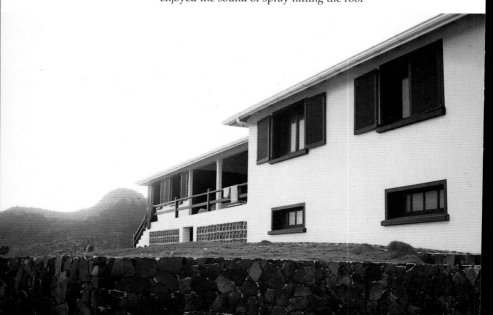

Cheery days on St Barts. Later, Rudolf took a fancy to my pink shorts and got them by throwing a fit of rage. This picture is a good gauge of his height; I am six foot one

See the eyes? Nureyev didn't much like me snapping him. Too intrusive. This is on St Barts, after breakfast. He's thinking about going to the beach and also thinking I'm wasting his time with this 'shit-camera'

Picture taken on St Barts by anonymous passer-by, betrayed by his shadow. The car was a gift from Rudolf's New York agent. Rudolf looks pensive. I look relieved, because he's just given me the car keys. He was the worst driver in the world

Rudolf and Bach on St Barts. He was so intent on the music that he was oblivious to the click of the camera. Occasionally he asked me to dust the keyboard, but never the whole piano. A rare hatless shot

Lunch outside at St Barts: chicken and salad, very simple. Rudolf is without his shawl – it must have been *very* hot. He was getting annoyed: 'Stop taking shit-photo and come and eat!'

Grand Saline was the nudist beach on St Barts, and Rudolf spent a lot of time there, swimming, studying orchestral scores, strolling, observing. He was still physically strong, but his body was in decline. The golden days were over

Rudolf's seafront place on St Barts. In the distance behind it is the headland where he swam (against my advice and beyond his ability) in great surges of surf. The thrill of being in the sea's control excited him

Uros Lajovic was big and strong and tough, and in Vienna he taught Rudolf a lot about the art of conducting. Lajovic worked him hard. Then Papa Hubener (right) took him home for – aptly – steak tartare

This is Rudolf at his very best, having fun at the Hubeners' summer-house after a lesson with the baton. Someone gave him the folding motorbike, and I carried it all over Europe for him. He always seemed about to fall off it, but he never did

Summer 1991: Rudolf eases into his new career. The first rehearsal is at Wilhelm (Papa) Hubener's summer-house outside Vienna. Rudolf conducts Mozart with Papa (violin), Ilse Wincor (violin) and Howard Penny (cello). Elisabeth Hubener checks the score. All quite informal, but Rudolf was very tense. Note the big teacup, always within reach

Rudolf's Mediterranean island of Li Galli, seen from the western tip. The path leads up to Rudolf's villa. Mainland Italy lies beyond. Li Galli was really just a rugged chunk of rock. Despite the large and hungry mosquitoes which bred in the many nooks and crannies, Li Galli satisfied Rudolf. He enjoyed isolation

Rudolf's bath on Li Galli. Stretched out in the tub, he could see Positano (on the mainland) through one door, and then turn his head and see Capri through another. He enjoyed that

A little day music on Li Galli. Howard Penny plays it as he thinks Mozart meant. Rudolf, with tea and score, concedes the point with a shrug. Amadeus, the builder's son, is in no doubt

On the boat from Li Galli to Capri. This is a very typical pose: beautifully relaxed yet slightly wary. Note the ever-present hat, the hotel towel (stolen), and the yellow clogs. When he lost a clog I offered to buy a new pair and he was touchingly pleased

This shot was taken after we went to a dinner party on Capri. Someone had rashly referred to the West's defeat of Hitler. Not so! Rudolf declared. The big battles were in the east – Russia suffered most and achieved most! (Military historians agree.) Rudolf is looking very Russian here

8

St Barts

Margot Calling Long-distance and Jackie for Tea

There were two ways into St Barts. You could fly in, which was often terrifying, or you could arrive by boat, which was sometimes merely grim.

St Barts airport is too small to take the big jets. These land on the island of St Martin and you finish your journey in a little island-hopper plane; but even for the island-hoppers, St Barts airstrip presents problems. It is boxed in by hills on three sides, with the sea on the fourth. When the wind blows from the right direction the plane makes its approach from the sea. Otherwise the pilot has to come in over the hills and lose height in a hurry. Come in too low and your undercarriage might hit cars driving along the hilltops. Come in too high and you might overshoot and end in the sea. Both these things happened (to different planes) while we were there.

Rudolf hated flying. He told me that when he and Margot Fonteyn were on tour in the Far East, their plane flew into an electrical storm and dropped like a stone. The plane got tossed around so violently, they were convinced they would never come out alive. After that, any flying – even in a jumbo jet on a calm day – was an ordeal. He had walked out of Paris airport not because he was tired but because he was scared. And when we missed our connecting flight at New York and got to St Martin too late to catch the island-hopper to St Barts, I'm sure he was relieved to be able to go by boat instead. The sea was very bumpy, and the boat was only a fifty-foot motor launch, but anything was better than bloody flying.

Rudolf went into the cabin. I stayed outside, in the stern cockpit. The trip took an hour and a half. As we lurched through the night people began to be sick. Eventually Rudolf joined me. He too was sick. Diesel fumes added to the rough sea, and he lost his airline dinner. He looked terrible. After a while, he threw up everything else he had eaten. This was a new view of the maestro. He lay with his head on my lap, as weak as a child. The man could be an egotistical monster, but he also aroused great feelings of protectiveness. I was worried about the spray that kept hitting him. 'You're getting soaked,' I said. 'Shall we go below'?'

'No. Don't mind spray as long as I get air.'

I had to help him ashore. He looked drained, which was understandable: there couldn't have been much left inside him. He was nothing if not resilient; next day he bounced back to his usual demanding and intolerant self. But why in God's name did he buy a house on St Barts when it was such a pain to get there? The answer lies in the question. When Nureyev wasn't in New York or Paris, he wanted to be somewhere remote. Sometimes he wondered aloud about moving to the island of Mustique, which was even more remote than St Barts. But Mustique was a lot smaller, and he might not be able to escape from his friends.

Nureyev had many friends and he didn't like them very much. He liked solitude. I spoiled his perfect solitude because he had to have somebody to cook for him and do complicated technical jobs like changing lightbulbs or driving cars. One of me was enough. There was never going to be a staff of more than one.

St Barts was just big enough – about five miles long – for Nureyev to have an isolated house, far from the town and next to the sea. It was a long, airy bungalow: two buildings with a roof over the space between them. By contrast with the Dakota and the quai Voltaire, this was just a simple summerhouse with nothing worth stealing: no paintings, no statues, no harpsichords. There was plenty of dusty junk lying around. The dust blew in from the beach. Rudolf wasn't houseproud. If something needed protection, it had a cover on it. There were many covers. When the trade winds blew, the waves hit the rocks and spray splashed the tiled roof. He liked that.

Nobody bothered him. The French influence is still strong on St Barts, and its people are courteous and laid-back. Famous faces come and go but there's never any hassle. He liked that too.

Above all, he liked the house because he could walk out of it and into the sea, and swim – always naked – in its swirling effervescence. Even the sea urchins didn't discourage him. When he walked across the rocks he invariably trod on one or two, and later I had to take the spines out of his feet. Not poisonous but painful, and for a dancer quite a price to pay. Oddly enough, Rudolf never learned to swim properly. He did a sort of ambitious dog-paddle.

The sea's energy fascinated him. Sometimes he swam when the sea was, in my opinion, dangerously big. On land he pulled his shawl around himself against the gentlest breeze; in the sea he could be downright reckless. There was a headland near the house, quite steep, with a path running around it. Rudolf thought it might be good for a stroll. I checked it out and told him it was too dangerous. Waste of breath. We set off. I wore trainers; he wore clogs. We climbed over boulders twice my height and eventually scrambled down to a platform shelf, covered in slippery weed. Every now and then the sea surged in and flooded the shelf and washed back out. Rudolf decided to swim. I said it was a bad idea. More wasted breath.

He plopped in. The surges swept him back and forth, in and out. He doggy-paddled as best he could, but it was obvious that he was mostly out of control. The sea was in command. That, of course, was what he enjoyed. In the end his dancer's instinct saved him. He timed a big surge perfectly and let it decant him, quite gracefully, on the shelf.

So he got away with it, and very smug it made him. At dinner parties he bragged about the expedition, and tried to wind me up in front of the guests: 'Blue was so nagging . . . Wahh-wahh-wahh. No fun. Dull dull dull. Eh, Blukes?' He might easily have broken a leg on that shelf, in which case I would have had to get him out of the water and carry him back along the path. No fun, that. Very dull dull dull. But there was no point in saying so. Nureyev always had to win every conversation. He liked to spar, but he always had to win. People who challenged his remarks were blacklisted: 'They bin mean to me.' If listeners were passive or non-committal, that (in his opinion) confirmed his rightness and raised his status, and so he carried on chatting. But any crossed words were unacceptable, and several times we left parties very abruptly because he wasn't winning a discussion.

After his swim on (and off) the shelf, Rudolf sat on a rock and began talking of building a house on that very spot. Nothing came of it. He already had builders making improvements to the bungalow (he had no planning permission, which was typical). I made other improvements: he told me to convert a rock pool into a bathing pool by rolling small boulders and lumps of coral into the sea. Unfortunately a week later the sea had rolled them all back.

'Maybe we use dynamite,' Rudolf said. 'Are there mines here? Where we obtain dynamite?'

The pool was twenty feet from the house. 'A bit risky, Rudolf,' I said. He dropped the idea.

When it came to property, he could afford to think big. When it came to buying nail clippers, he couldn't afford even to think about it. The difference was that he really needed nail clippers.

Robert Tracy had come down from New York to spend Christmas with us. That was good: he knew Rudolf's quirks and all the no-go areas, something I was still learning. He also knew that Rudolf couldn't cut his own toenails. Like most veteran dancers, Rudolf had hard, lumpy toenails, and it took someone with sharp and powerful clippers to trim them. One day Robert suggested that his nails were getting long.

'Yes. Find some clippers.'

'I haven't any. Do you, Blue?'

I didn't. My fingernail clippers weren't nearly strong enough.

'OK,' Robert said. 'We'll go and buy some.'

Rudolf said, 'We haven't enough money to buy toenail clippers.' And that was that. End of discussion. The peasant had spoken for the maestro. Robert and I bought some clippers out of the grocery money, and I cut Rudolf's toenails. Rudolf said nothing. As long as his problems were solved, he didn't care how it was done. It was one of many occasions when the world revolved around Nureyev.

But to understand Nureyev and money you have to

remember always that he had worked for every cent he owned, and was especially proud of the *manner* of his success. 'Everything I've earned is through dancing,' he told me. Baryshnikov had sold his name to a fashion designer label (which flopped). Rudolf had no time for that sort of thing. 'Everything is *me*. You should work for what you get.'

Nureyev's work-rate had always been phenomenal. At his best – and he stayed at his best for much of his thirty years in the West – he gave at least two hundred performances a year and he was paid at least ten thousand dollars a performance; often more. At that rate he was earning over two million dollars a year.

Even at the end of his career he commanded big fees. I know because sometimes I collected his pay. He sent me to the theatre and the manager handed me an envelope stuffed full of banknotes. Even megastars like to get paid in cash. Show business is precarious: companies fail, theatres burn down, impresarios go bust. In any case, the performer may be in another continent tomorrow. Nothing beats hard cash in the pocket.

Yet money was always a problem for Rudolf. Having made his millions, he was schizophrenic in his attitude to the stuff. He valued it as a symbol of his success, as enduring proof of his triumph. But money is worthless unless it's used, and he never really enjoyed handing it over. What was guaranteed to upset him was the need to take cash out of his wallet to pay unexpected bills, such as tuning the piano at St Barts.

The piano tuner travelled from island to island. He wasn't cheap, but he wasn't as expensive as, say, a bundle of dynamite to blast out the pool; and Rudolf had been ready to pay for that without blinking. While the man was working on the piano, Rudolf sat in another room, brooding. 'How much does it cost to tune a piano, Blue?'

He was asking the wrong person, of course, but he could-n't bring himself to ask the piano tuner. Like a lot of famously rich people, he suspected that he was being ripped off by suppliers who thought he wouldn't notice the difference. The thought of haggling with the piano tuner made him very uncomfortable. The thought of being over-charged made him acutely anxious. In the end he took out some money. 'Will this do?'

The tuner and I agreed a fair price. I went back and told Rudolf. It caused a sharp sucking-in of breath. 'Oh . . . that's a lot. To tune a piano? It's just a tweak. . . .' He was kidding himself: that piano had taken a beating. For a moment he didn't want to part with his money. Then he said, 'Oh well . . . the piano's good now.'

Once the pain of payment was over, he was pleased. But Nureyev never spent money on anything he could get free. He never had any personal stationery; all letters and faxes got written on hotel stationery which he acquired on his travels. He never bought a toothbrush; he always cleaned his teeth with a giveaway hotel toothbrush. And when we flew from Paris to St Martin, he told me to pocket the Air France cutlery. If it wasn't nailed down, Nureyev took it. If it was loosely nailed down, he took it and the nail too. You never know when you might need a nail.

And yet no dancer worked harder to make money, or spent it more lavishly. What made working for him so diffi-cult was his habit of assuming that someone else would pay the bill. Later, when we were back at the Dakota, this habit almost got me fired. He decided to go to a dance studio. I had work to do in the apartment. We went out and I stopped a taxi. He said, 'Money? You got money for taxi?'

All I had was a hundred dollar bill, for housekeeping. His fuse began to burn. I searched my pockets. 'You

71

must. . . .' he said. 'Go and get. . . .' Already he was almost speechless with fury. I was wasting his time. 'Forget it!' He set off down West 72nd Street. The studio was a mile and a half away. I chased after him, got change, got another taxi. 'You must prepare these things,' he said bleakly.

After that I never went anywhere without a pocketful of change: dollars, pounds, francs, lire, Austrian schillings. There is a story about the Queen of England: she never looks behind her when she sits down, because she knows that someone will always be there with a chair. Rudolf had the same attitude towards the minor costs of living: someone would always be there with a handful of cash.

And yet . . . there were bound to be occasions when there would be no escape for him. If we were travelling, just the two of us, then he'd have to pay. He always carried his money in a wallet in the inside pocket of his big, dark-green raincoat. This never left him. He liked to feel the reassuring weight of the wallet, but in a curious way he didn't quite trust himself with the money inside it. Restaurant bills made him especially unhappy.

For a start, the currency usually baffled him. He understood dollars, but if we were outside America – for instance, in Italy – he'd pass me the bill and say, 'How much is that?'

'That's sixty-five thousand lire, Rudolf. About forty dollars.'

'Ah. OK.'

But it wasn't OK, because he wasn't sure what sixty-five thousand lire looked like. He took his coat from the back of his chair, unbuttoned the inside pocket and took out his wallet. As he did this, he turned his body away from me and used his shoulder to hide his actions while he took some notes out. Then he showed me. 'Is that. . . ?'

'That's a hundred thousand lire, Rudolf. So you want thirty-five thousand back.'

Now the agony really began. He had to reckon the tip. When the change came he was thoroughly miserable. He picked notes up, put some back, dithered and fiddled and suddenly said, 'Forget it, come on, let's go.'

Rudolf never understood tipping. He never really understood money. He could buy a house but he jibbed at buying a toothbrush. In that restaurant, it would have been much easier if he'd given the money to me and told me to pay; but he couldn't.

Rudolf had grown up in the Russian city of Ufa. When he first went to kindergarten he was barefoot; his family could not afford shoes for him. After all these years, mentally he was still barefoot. He didn't trust me, or anyone. You can take the boy out of Ufa, but you can't take Ufa out of the boy.

There was something wrong with a day if Rudolf couldn't have what's called a class (because several dancers usually practise together) and what he called a scrape (because it involved scraping his feet on the floor). All he needed was a smooth surface, such as a piece of Formica, and a kitchen chair to hold onto. Then by amazing good luck, I found a ballet studio on St Barts. It had been built for a girls' school: thirty feet square, a barre around the walls, a long mirror and a sprung floor. It was perfect for his daily scrape. This was a routine he'd followed for over thirty years. It made the heart pump the blood vigorously to all parts, it reminded those parts exactly how they should move, and it set him up for the rest of the day. The scrape was a kind of duel between Rudolf's mind and his body. His mind knew what it wanted, and it wasn't going to leave until his body obeyed orders. This took between fifty and sixty minutes. When it seemed that he was almost finished, I'd ask if he wanted a towel? Should I fetch the car?

73

'No. I want to do this one.'

He wasn't going to quit until he'd got it right. He'd try the step again and again, seeking to capture something that was evading him, until – bingo! it worked. His body had come up trumps. He'd be wet with sweat and ready for a plunge in the sea.

The rest of the day was ninety-five per cent routine. What made it interesting was the odd five per cent which was made up of totally unpredictable shocks and surprises.

On a typical day, Rudolf bashed away at the piano – always Bach – and then put his clogs on and strolled out, often in my clothes, to the patio. He ate lunch, bashed some more Bach, had a scrape and a plunge and a nap, and ate dinner. There was no lack of international phone calls, some from Margot Fonteyn, most from people who wanted him to dance or direct or choreograph. But Rudolf had come to St Barts to escape all that. He was relaxed, living at half-pace. That made him twice as fast as me. He called me 'Death'.

Shopping in St Barts meant driving a couple of miles to town, buying fresh stuff in the market and driving home. I didn't waste any time. When I walked in he'd be playing the piano. 'Aah ... *death*,' he'd say. He could stretch the word like chewing gum. 'Here comes *death*. You take so long. I think I'll send you out to get Death. Then you'll never come back! And I'll be happy. ...' And he'd go on playing.

Nureyev never let up on this mockery of what he considered my plodding slowness. It didn't make working for him any easier: after all, why rush? If he was on St Barts to rest, what was so urgent about bringing home the shopping? Pleasing Nureyev wasn't just hard; it was impossible. I could never move or think fast enough for him.

Like most people I thought in hours and minutes. He was a dancer; he thought in seconds and microseconds. In his world, anyone who wasn't dancing was plodding. An example of this was his favourite breakfast, scrambled eggs. The first time I made it, he took a bite and said, 'Two seconds more and it would have been perfect.' He wasn't joking, and when he said two seconds he meant precisely that.

As F. Scott Fitzgerald said, the very rich are different from you and me. Even on St Barts, you can't always pick up the phone and call them. Rudolf told me to telephone an important estate agent. 'I understand Mrs Onassis is on the island,' I said to the man. 'Can you get a message to her to call Rudolf Nureyev?'

'If she wants to call you,' the man said politely, 'she will call you.'

Which she did, five minutes later. And came around for a cup of tea.

When she closed the car door and turned to look at us, it was hard not to recoil a little in disbelief. Here was one of the faces that symbolized the second half of the twentieth century. You see so many pictures that the reality comes as a shock: a media event come to life, walking forward, smiling at Rudolf, being introduced to me, making sure she got my name. 'Blue? How d'you do.' I went off and made tea.

Rudolf and Jackie went back a long way. They had met in 1963, during the Royal Ballet's American tour, when she'd invited Margot Fonteyn and Rudolf to the White House. Now they had many mutual friends, and the conversation flowed. None of it was enormously important but all of it was fun, and at the end they agreed to have dinner. There was a terrible moment when Rudolf suggested that Jackie should bring her family to dinner at his house; this would have meant that I cooked. It would also have meant getting money out of Rudolf. The crisis passed: Jackie had already booked a table at *La Banane*.

It turned out to be quite a party: her son and daughter were there, and some friends. Jackie sat opposite Rudolf and next to me. When she was the First Lady, gossip columnists and cartoonists had portrayed her as something of a Barbie doll. They got her wrong. She was intelligent, quick and clever. She was also remarkably easy to talk to. She soon found out that I'd sailed across the Pacific.

'Wow! Fantastic thing to do. John, did you hear what Blue did? Isn't that courageous?' John was about to take his law exams. He didn't seem to share his mother's enthusiasm. I enjoyed it. Jackie Onassis was one of those people who make you feel that maybe you've underrated yourself.

The meal began well. The chat bounced back and forth. Rudolf was very relaxed. He could make people laugh with his one-liners, which were always on the edge of being outrageous, and that's what gossip is about. Then, as the evening wore on, he started going over the edge. It was the difference between the first glass of wine and the second. His humour became slightly crude. The cruder it got, the drunker he got. His remarks were becoming clumsy, and that wasn't funny. Jackie took it in her stride, but I could see some of the younger Kennedys looking sideways at Rudolf, wondering: *Is there going to be a scene?* It wasn't that he enjoyed getting drunk; quite the opposite. He simply had a very low tolerance for alcohol. (There were times when he took a glass of white wine and behaved as if he'd had five pints of lager.) John and Caroline and their friends were bored and uncomfortable. They weren't happy alongside this tipsy queer, even if he was a friend of their mother's, and they weren't sure what to make of me, the queer's side-kick. But Jackie – elegant, warm and attentive – kept the evening moving along. She was amazing.

In the car afterwards, Rudolf was silent. Sober, he was a good talker; drunk, he was inclined to be pompous. After a while he said something about Jackie's strength, and their friendship 'Both our losses,' he said. 'Me and my country. Her and her husband.' Silence. Then, 'My houses are very solitary. Like wolves' lairs.' I let it pass. Wolves' lairs may be remote but they're not solitary; they're full of wolves. But if he felt like being a wolf, let him be a wolf.

Next afternoon there was a short postscript to the Jackie Onassis dinner. It was John Kennedy's birthday; he was planning to go body surfing. I offered to take him surfing instead. I got some boards; we met at the beach; I ran through the basics; we paddled out. The surf wasn't great. I caught a couple of waves; he caught none and his frustration bred a kind of grim obstinacy. At dusk I paddled out and said we should call it a day. He refused. I surfed in. It grew darker, and he was still out there. Enough Kennedys had died; I didn't want to be responsible for losing another at sea, so I paddled out again. Meanwhile he caught half a wave and ended on a reef, twenty yards out. By the time we got to the beach, his city feet were cut and he was cursing loud and hard. (My feet were like leather.) All in all, the afternoon had not been good for his image. We shook hands, and he shot off. Neither of us was sorry to see the back of the other. And none of this would be worth recording, except that an hour later, Jackie was on the phone. Was I all right? How were my feet? Had I cut myself? Thanks for looking after John.

She didn't have to do that. Who was I? Just Rudi's gofer. But she did it.

Then it was back to routine: waking before he did, so as to be ready for his whistle; cooking and cleaning and laundry;

reminding him to take his pill; fetching and carrying. Driving. Grand Saline is the fashionable nudist beach on St Barts, and Rudolf went there a lot. I drove. Once there, he stripped off, sat in the sand and conducted Beethoven and Bach.

He was launching himself on a second career as a conductor. Third, if you counted a couple of movies that flopped (*Valentino, Exposed*) and a spell on the boards in *The King and I*. He knew he couldn't dance much longer; anybody else would have quit dancing years ago. Leonard Bernstein and Herbert von Karajan had each, separately, told him to take up conducting because, as Bernstein had said, 'Conductors live a long, long time.' Many do. Lenny was dead, but only after living a rich, full life, and Rudolf was encouraged by this.

I had bought Rudolf a waterproof Walkman that was safe from sand and salt. He wore a hat and the headphones and nothing else and listened to symphonies while he followed the score on sheet music that was so old and tattered that pages often blew away. His hand ticked off the bars like a metronome and he muttered *tsum, tsum, tsum, tsum, tsum* in a deep voice. He was almost, but not quite, in a world of his own. If a good-looking young buck wandered into his vision, he enjoyed the view. He might even abandon Beethoven and go for a stroll to check out the talent. But that was where it ended. A friend of his, Bob Colacello, has been quoted as saying that Rudolf looked 'magnificent' on that beach. Well, magnificence is in the eye of the beholder. I couldn't see it. Without a leotard and an orchestra, his body was nothing to flaunt. His face could still stop people in their tracks, but the line of the body had gone. Thinning hair, a wrinkled neck, a slightly saggy chest, a thickening at the waist, extremely battered feet – nothing could disguise the advance of age. Very seldom did young men approach him. He liked it when it happened. 'Aaaaaah,' he'd say, 'pretty boys.' Then he went back to the oblivion of his Walkman.

Wearing headphones makes you deaf to the outside world. One day I brought a picnic lunch. He'd asked for soft-boiled eggs, so I'd soft-boiled them and wrapped them in foil. When he unwrapped one and took a bite, he roared in a voice that turned heads a hundred yards away: '*You didn't think there were any rocks on this beach so you brought your own.*'

Then, back to the score. *Tsum, tsum, tsum, tsum, tsum.*

Nobody was obliged to be naked on Grand Saline beach, but most people were. I always wore shorts or Speedos, not because I disliked being nude but because it helped to define the relationship between us. By now we each knew what we expected of the other. Rudolf was an artist – a brilliant, elusive, secretive, fast-thinking, impatient, intolerant individual. I was a mechanic: a solid, reliable, hard-working, straight Anglo-Saxon. Once he realized that I wasn't going to be a quick fuck, then he saw that I could be a useful asset, for the very reason that I was not going to be emotional baggage. He needed someone to bring a little stability to his life.

On his side, Rudolf's judgement of me (as of everyone) was fast and astute. I was no gamble. He hadn't signed my contract. He'd made it clear from the start that I was free to leave any time I wasn't happy, without giving notice, just as he was free to tell me to go whenever he felt I was a burden. If I wanted security it was up to me to take out insurance. Although we shared the same house, ate together, travelled together, he wanted to remain distant.

On my side I worked hard to retain a sense of order and stability when the only certain thing was constant change. That was why I tried to behave correctly, in every sense. At

Grand Saline, I wore shorts. Always, when I spoke, I used good English: never 'I'm gonna make lunch': always 'I'm going to make lunch'. And most importantly, I kept my language clean. Rudolf swore a lot (as most dancers do). I have nothing against swearing, but by not swearing I confirmed the difference between his role and mine, and I helped to maintain the all-important sense of calm and competence. The value of this approach was shown on the only occasion, in my whole year with Rudolf, when I swore. Whoever had wired the toaster in the kitchen at St Barts must have been colour-blind. It gave me a shock that flung me across the room, and I bawled: '*Fuuuuck!*' Rudolf was worried: anything that made me swear must be extremely serious. I was somewhat wobbly. He asked if I wanted some water – a measure of his concern, since he was usually indifferent to other people's pain and suffering. I apologized for my language.

That incident was the exception that proved the rule. Standards must be maintained – for both our sakes. Living with Rudolf demanded total self-control. Usually his behaviour was balanced and calm, but at any moment it might suddenly go ballistic.

Rudolf liked watching CNN. That meant getting a satellite dish which, on St Barts, wasn't easy. I shopped in the morning, took him to the beach and spent the whole afternoon at the TV shop, trying to sort out the problems. When I got home I was hot, sticky and tired. I hadn't stopped working since I'd got up. Rudolf was sitting on the patio, catching the last of the sun. 'OK?' he said.

'It's not an instant fix, Rudolf. It's going to take a while to get the stuff here.'

He frowned. This was not what he wanted to hear. When Nureyev orders CNN, he wants CNN *now*. 'Time for dinner,' he said.

'Quick shower. Then I'll get in the kitchen.'

'Cook dinner.'

'D'you mind if I have a shower?'

Rudolf leaped out of his sun bed, stepped up close to me, and screamed; '*I DON'T WORK FOR YOU! YOU WORK FOR ME!*'

Ignition, lift-off, impact, overkill. All in the blink of an eye.

Christ, I thought, what have I done now? I've been belting around all day, I'm sweaty and grimy, I just want to clean up so I can cook his meal, and he's gone mad. When Nureyev went off the rails it was never anything less than a howling disaster. 'I'm very sorry,' I said. It was essential to calm him down. I put a hand on his shoulder. 'I'll go and make dinner now.'

All of a sudden he was exhausted. 'Please don't make me angry like that,' he said. 'Make dinner. Have shower after.' He sounded flat, empty. Later that evening he said, 'You're very good for me, Blue. But you're so slow. You're like Death.' All was forgiven – for the moment.

Most days were uneventful, and life was pleasant. One night we had dinner at *La Banane*, and the waiter said, 'Have you enjoyed your meal, sir?' and Rudolf said, 'No, I didn't enjoy. Blue can cook better.' Exit the waiter. Rudolf always gave a straight answer. His philosophy was: If you can't take the answer, don't ask the question. So I suppose my cooking must have improved. We usually ate at home. Occasionally Rudolf would watch a video and gossip about the stars he had known. He liked epic movies, especially *Lawrence of Arabia*.

'I knew Peter O'Toole,' he said. 'He drank so much. Once he drank until five in the morning. Then woke me and said: Buy me a taxi. Of course my day was ruined.' It's significant that what stuck in Rudolf's mind was his broken night. Dancers must sleep; there is no substitute for rest. When

Rudolf was dancing, the only party he went to was on the last night, when it didn't matter.

He remembered another legendary drinker, Richard Burton: 'God, he used to bore us at dinner with poetry. His own. On and on! God!'

I mentioned Olivier and Gielgud.

'John Gielgud was a very kind man. Gay, of course. But polite. Great actor.'

I waited for a comment about Olivier, but nothing came. Which could mean something. Or nothing.

When we reached St Barts from Paris, Rudolf had no car there – cars are expensive on the island – so Andrew Grossman gave him one. It was a small Japanese model. I picked it up at the showroom and drove it home. 'I'd like to try it,' Rudolf said.

There was a short driveway leading to his house. He turned the key, gunned the engine and we shot down the drive. He stamped on the brakes and snatched at the gearstick, then he stamped on the gas. The springs didn't know which way to go. He made the car kangaroo halfway across the island. He got the maximum noise out of every part except the radio. He was the worst driver I have ever seen.

He pulled over and stopped. He seemed satisfied with the car's performance, and with his own. 'Mmmm! Good car.' Short pause. 'You drive.'

He never drove it again. Thank God.

Luigi was right: Nureyev was a unique individual. It was not only dangerous to apply conventional standards to him, it was pointless. A reasonable person might say that he had behaved unreasonably over that business of the shower and the meal, but a reasonable person would never have achieved what Nureyev achieved. He didn't live in a rational world; he lived in a world where fantasy ruled and where the price you paid for artistic genius was artistic temperament. Ordinary people live lives of compromise. We constantly adjust to each others' needs. That, we believe, is the civilized way to behave. Nureyev didn't. Nureyev had only one belief: he believed in Nureyev. That was what had got him out of a Russian backwater and raised him over a vast array of obstacles that would have defeated anyone without Nureyev's total and passionate certainty that he was the greatest dancer in the world. He turned out to be right, and that justified his making the rules. All the rules. When he behaved selfishly or foolishly or inconsiderately or just plain badly, those were the judgements of other people who didn't live in his world, and so their opinions were meaningless because these people were not Nureyev. It wasn't that Nureyev broke all the rules and didn't care. Nureyev didn't recognize anybody else's rules. They never entered his mind.

Nureyev could seem self-destructive. It was impossible to work for him without thinking: *This man's life would be a lot easier if only he would behave more reasonably.* But to think like that was to miss the point. If Nureyev had behaved reasonably he would never have been Nureyev. His genius was the only justification he needed. That's why living with him was not easy. It was unforgettable, but it was not easy.

Christmas 1990 was a curious time. Two of Rudolf's former lovers came to stay with him at St Barts, and Rudolf himself spent Christmas with an old admirer in Paris. It was an odd arrangement but it worked.

Rudolf's one-night stands had been legion, but as far as I knew only three long-term lovers figured in his life. He met Erik Bruhn soon after he defected. Bruhn was Danish, a great classical dancer and an international star at a time when Nureyev was still establishing himself. He was also ten years older, and a heavy drinker and smoker. (He died – officially of lung cancer – in 1986, at the age of fifty-eight.) Rudolf and Erik were a fixture for much of the sixties, which were a very rich time for Rudolf: he told me that he was simultaneously in love with Erik, Margot and Fred – Sir Frederick Ashton, the Royal Ballet's top choreographer. Maybe he meant it; maybe he was just trying to surprise me. He spoke little about Erik. He did recall his heavy smoking, and his unattractive habit of correcting Rudolf's bad English in public. What he remembered best was an occasion when a hotel maid suddenly opened the door to their room at a moment when they were on the bed, in the nude, thoroughly enjoying each other's company. 'Just checking!' the maid piped, totally unconcerned, and closed the door. It was a favourite remark of Rudolf's. Whenever somebody blundered, he piped up, 'Just checking!'

Wallace Potts came on the scene after Erik. He was a tall, amiable American, very easy-going, with a fine, wry sense of humour. In the seventies Rudolf had a house in East Sheen, a leafy suburb of London, and they spent a lot of time there. Maude Gosling (who helped and befriended Rudolf from the time he first came to London) told me that he and Wallace used to wrestle and throw each other in the air with great gusto: more like teenagers than young men, she said. Everyone liked Wallace; he was great fun. He hadn't much money, so Rudolf paid for him and his dogs to fly down from New York. (No money for nail clippers but money for airline tickets.) Rudolf liked to play with the dogs, especially a big black mutt called Mike.

Rudolf's third and final lover was, of course, Robert Tracy. I was glad to see him again; he knew how to read Rudolf's moods, how to go with the flow. And quite soon we needed all of Robert's skill.

Wallace's brother joined us. He was brash. He talked too much and thought too little before he spoke. For instance, he expected me to unpack his bags. When that didn't happen, he made his feelings known. Rudolf had to tell him that I wasn't everybody's valet and that he'd have to do his own unpacking. Later, the brother wanted a drink. Whatever it was – beer or scotch – we had none. His tone of voice suggested that he was disappointed that Rudolf had failed to provide a full range of drinks. Rudolf blew up in a rage. I drove the brother to the liquor store while Robert and Wallace did a calm-down job on Rudolf, something they were experienced at. The brother didn't stay long.

When the three of us concentrated on maintaining a tranquil atmosphere, free from hassle, Rudolf remained on an even keel. He and Wallace were on affectionate terms. They had single beds in Rudolf's bedroom, but it seems unlikely that they were lovers in the physical sense. The house was not big, and Wallace and Robert were good friends. If Rudolf and Wallace had been lovers while Robert was in the next bedroom, a certain tension would have been inevitable.

The vibes in general were relaxed and pleasant. They had all known each other for years, and they understood their relationships better than I ever could. After Wallace left, I embarrassed Rudolf and Robert one evening. The kitchen was beyond the television room. I went to get a glass of water and found them watching some painful-looking buggery on a porn video. (Rudolf took porn videos with him wherever he went.) They were disconcerted. I apologized and left. We were all in one house, but they had their world and I had mine.

Nureyev had little time for religion. He was a Tartar, born into a Muslim family, but he didn't practise that or any other faith. Once, as he wandered by, he paused to say, 'I don't think the Bible should be taken as fact. How God shits. All the angels and stuff.' Then he wandered on. It was the only time that he mentioned religion. (His funeral ceremony took place in the Palais Garnier, which is the theatre of Paris Opéra.)

Close to Christmas time, he called New York from St Barts, got through to Columbia Artists International, and asked for Andrew Grossman. They asked who was calling. 'Rudolf,' he said. Long pause. It was obvious that the name alone meant nothing to the person at the other end. Rudolf who? He turned on his very deep voice.

'Rooo-dolf! Red Fucking Nose Reindeer!'

Amazingly, that worked. He got through to Grossman. So, for a while, he used it all the time. He would call Paris: 'Ah! This Red Nose! How you going?'

Then he decided to spend Christmas in Paris. His host or hostess must have been hugely rich or delightful or influential, or all three, to get him onto an aeroplane. On the morning of the flight, he had a bad case of twitch. He was pulling stuff from his bag as I was packing it. I was folding his clothes, he was throwing them on the floor. It was a green canvas bag, the kind that folds over to make it a carry-on job. He was only going for a few days. The question was: could I pack it faster than he could unpack it?

In the end he stopped trying. He knew he had to go. I drove him to the airport. We walked together across the tarmac. When we reached the aircraft door he was shaking. At this rate he wouldn't get up the steps. Something had to be done to distract him from the sight of that terrifying island-hopper. I had my British passport with a photograph taken when I was nineteen. It's the worst bad-passport-photo in the world. As he reached the aircraft steps, I said, 'Rudolf', and showed him the picture. He laughed. He went up the steps and they closed the door behind him. Mission accomplished.

It sounds juvenile, even infantile. The point is, it worked. It helped get Rudolf over the worst part of the ordeal, which was climbing aboard the machine. At that awful moment he could respond only to the very simplest communication, such as a comic picture. He was like a child.

I met him at the airport when he came back from Paris. It was hot, even for St Barts; I was in shorts and a T-shirt. Rudolf got off the island-hopper wearing a full-length sable fur coat. He had worn it all the way. He kept it on until we got home. Evidently his Paris admirer was very appreciative. And Rudolf was feeling the cold more than ever.

Sometimes I answered the phone and it would be Margot Fonteyn, calling Rudolf from a hospital in the southern United States. It was a strange experience, being the link – however brief – between the principals of one of the greatest love stories of the century. In the eyes of the world, Nureyev and Fonteyn went together like Romeo and Juliet (which they danced many times) but with one big difference: theirs was a long and happy story.

When they met, when they came together at the Royal Ballet in the early sixties, she was old enough to be his mother. And yet when they danced, it was as if they had been made for each other. This was before my time, but film of their performances has survived and there isn't a hint that their ages are wrong; quite the reverse. Often they succeeded in looking much *younger* than they were; at times they appear to be a couple of youngsters ignoring the law of gravity and having the most tremendous fun while they were at it. They had a love affair with ballet.

Whether they ever had a love affair off-stage is something we shall probably never know. It seems highly unlikely that they did, for two reasons. First, it would have been contrary to his sexual preference, and second, it would have been against her character.

Nureyev was an out-and-out homosexual. He liked some women, but the idea of having one as a long-term sexual partner bemused him. Much later, in 1991, on his island in the Mediterranean, when he was feeling relaxed after dinner, he raised the subject of marriage. 'I can't understand why you're so against women,' he said. This was the reverse of the truth, and he knew it, so he was winding me up; but it paid to tread cautiously when you disagreed with Nureyev. I said it was the prospect of marriage that I was unsure about, not women.

'Perhaps I should have married Margot. But I had many women, and it was like your aquatic salad.'

'Aquatic' meant 'sloppy': he reckoned I always put too much dressing on the salad. 'Bang-bang-bang,' he said, 'and there is a hip bone which bangs you in the dick.' With anybody else, I might have said that it sounded as if he'd been a bit off-target. As it was I made a non-committal noise and stacked the dishes. 'Do you enjoy sleeping with women?' he asked. I said I did. 'How can you do it?' he said, and he sounded genuinely baffled. 'Hammering away for hours and hours?' It was a rhetorical question. The conversation had gone on long enough. Nureyev liked short, sharp discussions. As I turned away I saw the moon rising from the sea, as red as rust.

'Hey,' I said. 'What a great moon.'

Rudolf made his voice low and theatrical. 'Great for buggery.'

On-stage, he was a great romantic. Off-stage, he could not appear to be the slightest bit romantic. Perhaps that was because he dared not give a part of himself to someone else;

he reserved all his emotional strength for ballet. Thus he could express his feelings totally when he was dancing a part, but as soon as he turned back into Nureyev he hid behind a mask of coarse indifference to anyone else. Total selfishness is never totally satisfying, but by now Nureyev was too old to change. Occasionally he revealed glimpses of vulnerability or of rage. Sometimes the vulnerability prompted the rage. But it all added up to a picture of a man who could never give himself to a woman because, at heart, he didn't want to.

His remark – 'Perhaps I should have married Margot' – begs the question whether Margot would have married him. There is no evidence that she wanted to, and for her to have had an affair with him seems completely out of character. The chemistry that draws couples together is beyond understanding, but Margot Fonteyn was the ultimate professional and it's hard to see her giving in to any self-indulgence that might distract her from ballet. What's more, although she was not without great passion, she had a very clear and very British sense of what was appropriate. Margot was married, and by all reports she was serious about marriage – far more serious than her husband was.

She was married to Robert Arias, a Panamanian diplomat. At one time he was ambassador to the Court of St James's. When Nureyev defected and came to stay with them, the house they lived in was the embassy, and by then she was Dame Margot Fonteyn. Robert – whom she called Tito – was a high-flyer: through him she met everyone from Sir Winston Churchill to Marilyn Monroe. Margot was what Americans call 'straight arrow'. It's hard to believe that Rudolf, for all his boyish charm and brilliance, could have seduced her from what she saw as her duty to Tito, especially when he got shot.

Even by South American standards, Panamanian politics

have always been dodgy. Tito had tried and failed to lead a revolution there. His political colleagues could forgive his political incompetence; what they couldn't overlook was his success with their wives. Tito made no attempt to hide this, which was particularly galling. In 1964 he was driving through Panama City. According to Rudolf, the wife of a politician called Jiminez was beside him. At a red light, Jiminez came over and pointed a revolver into the car and emptied it at Tito. He fired six shots. Three hit. The newspapers said it was all about politics. Rudolf said he knew better. A quarter of a century later he still brooded angrily over it.

'You know why he was shot?' he said to me. 'Because he was cheating on Margot. She was going to divorce him, and his friends shot him. They missed because they had such fury – shaking!' Rudolf acted out a gunman trembling with rage. 'She should have divorced him sooner.'

None of this rings true. If Jiminez didn't shoot Tito because he was getting screwed politically, he is far more likely to have done it because his wife was getting screwed regularly. For Rudolf to imagine that Tito's friends shot him 'because he was cheating on Margot' is to credit Panamanian politics with more chivalry than it deserves. But it says a lot about Rudolf. He could afford to nurse his resentment towards Tito, just as he could afford to wonder whether he should have married Margot ('Maybe it would have worked') because these were all memories, capable of being endlessly adjusted as the years went by. The notion of marriage with Margot was a pleasant dream: an extension of their gossamer partnership on stage, with the added appeal of the act of gallantry he might have performed in replacing the treacherous Tito. Marrying Margot was a harmless fantasy, just like the fantasies they had danced together. Rudolf enjoyed creating little fantasies, especially after dinner when he was a little drunk and was trying to scandalize me.

First he said he should have married Margot; then he said that she was a lesbian. He felt sure of this (he said) because he had seen her with somebody else's wife. It was a typical bit of Nureyev gossip. He talked about homosexuality as easily as other people talk about the weather. (Once – slightly drunk again – he even hinted that he might have had a homosexual relationship with Bobby Kennedy. Wishful thinking, perhaps.)

But when he was stone-cold sober he paid tribute to Margot's strength and skill, something he never said about any other dancer. In the very early days of their partnership they were due to dance a ballet that was new to him, and he was nervous. 'I can't do that,' he told her. 'I'll ruin it.'

'Just you try!' she said. He admired her unshakeable balance. When he was young he was too foul-mouthed and abrupt for his own good; she taught him a lot about tact and diplomacy, qualities that even a genius needs if he is to survive in the bitchy world of dance. Rudolf mentioned that when they were at the Royal Ballet, Sir Frederick Ashton murmured in his ear, 'See Margot off.' Now, Ashton had actually created a ballet especially for them, *Marguerite and Armand*. So what had he meant? See her off the stage?

'Yes. Keep dancing, hang in, dance longer than her. That's what Fred meant. Survive old bat.'

But in fact Margot went on dancing for many more years.

Rudolf had an expressive trick of hitching up an eyebrow. 'Very strong woman.'

He told the story of the blue movie. It was about men in prison. There were a lot of full-frontals, with raunchy scenes of oral sex. This was in the sixties, when the cinema was still very firmly censored. Rudolf was invited to a private showing. Also invited were Margot Fonteyn,

Margot's mother and Maude Gosling (married to the dance critic of the *Observer* and Rudolf's guardian angel).

'Was bit of mix-up,' Rudolf said. 'Nobody was sure what film was about.' Then it was projected. 'I held my breath . . . and right at end, Margot said, "Well! Wasn't that good?" She was great. Old-fashioned somewhat, but great.'

But even in her long career Margot Fonteyn couldn't make enough money to pay for her retirement. The three bullets that hit Tito left him semi-paralysed and near death. She brought him to Stoke Mandeville, probably the best hospital in the world for such cases. The doctors saved his life but nobody could reverse the paralysis. He lived for another twenty-five years, thanks to Margot's attention, and to her bank balance. When he died, in 1989, she was poor and dying of cancer on a small farm in Panama. One way or another, fit or helpless, Tito had got through nearly all her money. Rudolf was right: Margot was old-fashioned but great. Tito was the man she married, and after he was shot her loyalty to him was redoubled. She stuck it out to the end.

She never asked for help. Somehow, word of her plight reached the ballet world. In May 1990 Rudolf danced at a benefit gala at Covent Garden. It raised a quarter of a million pounds which created a trust fund that paid for Margot to go to a hospital in the US for treatment.

From there she had long telephone conversations with Rudolf. The house on St Barts was open-plan; it was almost impossible not to overhear his share of the conversation. When he hung up he seldom spoke of her, but a glance at his face showed how moved he was, and that was rare with Rudolf. Normally he put other people's suffering out of his mind. But then, Margot was very rare. He told me, 'She refuses to have medication until she phones me. Then has painkillers for rest of day.'

Knowing this, he worried about the length of their telephone calls. This produced a remark that sums up both their friendship and their greatness. Rudolf said, 'I should go. Or I tire you out.'

'Listen,' Margot said. 'You *never* tired me out. *Never.*'

Her strength and determination amazed him. 'Already she is making plans to go back to Panama. Nobody to look after her there, she will die of infection. I asked her, come here, but no.' And then one day she called him and she forgot where she was. Everything got jumbled in her mind. Rudolf just sat there, looking beaten down by sadness. 'I can't. . . .' he said. 'She's gone . . . I can't understand what she says or. . . .' I took the phone from his hand, and he walked away. Clinically Margot was still alive, but from that moment she had left him for ever.

Rudolf's cure for grief was work. There was another tour coming up and he had to stay fit. His body was in good shape, but there were minor ailments. He suffered from piles. The disorder itself didn't cause him much distress, but the buying of pile cream did. It was not something that Nureyev could do without the risk of gossip and maybe even scandal, so I bought the cream for him. Meanwhile, his doctor in Paris, Michel Canesi, kept up the supply of blue-and-white pills, and I kept reminding Rudolf to take one twice a day with meals, and he kept forgetting. When he went to Paris he invariably brought back at least half the pills he should have taken.

For his daily scrape I drove him to the studio, carrying towels and dance shoes and other clobber. Then I'd retire to the background and watch the maestro do his stuff.

One day he fell. Badly.

It was towards the end of the session. He wanted to practise a certain kind of pirouette. To help his feet turn more

93

easily, he sprinkled water on the floor. Something went wrong, the floor was too wet or his turn was too fast, he fell forwards and both knees hit the floor, with all his weight behind them. He was in great pain. When I reached him he was on all fours, looking up, and he had just enough breath to say, 'Oh shitttt . . . that hurt.'

I carried him to the car and drove him home. He'd already briefed me on exactly what to do. In the freezer we had a big bottle of high-proof vodka and a handtowel that had been wet when it was put in, so now it was frozen stiff. I soaked the towel in vodka and wrapped it around one knee. We should have had another frozen towel but we didn't, so I made a towel as cold as I could, soaked it in vodka, wrapped it around the other knee. I got two plastic garbage bags, tore them open and wrapped a bag around each knee, and fixed them so they wouldn't come off. By now it was late afternoon. Rudolf went to bed, wearing what was in effect a freezing cold compress around each knee. At midnight I replaced these compresses with fresh towels, fresh vodka.

In the morning his bedroom stank like the cheapest bar in Russia. Let no one tell you that vodka has no smell. The stuff we were using had come from Russia and it was as strong as paint-stripper. Rudolf never drank it. When the plastic bags came off, steam poured out of the towels. His knees were hot. The pain had gone. He didn't get up and dance, but the damage to his knees had been made good. The vodka cold-compress (which ends up as a hot compress) is a very old Russian method of treating bruised muscles. Rudolf learned of it at the Kirov Ballet. In Russia, if they can't get vodka, they use a liquid made from the flowers of a herb called arnica, which is good for bruises. Whisky is another alternative. But vodka is best.

'I was wondering,' he said.

It was late January 1991, we were just about to fly to New York, he would soon be starting another US tour with *Nureyev and Friends*. I'd packed all the bags. He said, 'Whether it would be difficult for you to stay here.'

Rudolf left, I stayed. He wanted me to oversee the builders working on the house. He didn't trust builders, they might slack. I was to keep them up to scratch, get them paid, call Rudolf every week, meet him in a month or so when the work was finished.

I checked out the contractors twice a day, stayed fit by running around the island (one lap equals fifteen miles) and went to parties. It was a piece of cake. A diet of cake gets boring after a while. Neil and Heather – with whom I'd crossed the Pacific – were getting married in England, and I was invited. I phoned Rudolf. He didn't like the idea.

'All I'm doing is watching builders put bricks on top of each other,' I said. 'They're not going to stop just because I'm not here. They know I'll be back soon.'

Rudolf still disliked the idea, but he hated arguments, and he especially hated arguments that were going on his phone bill. So I went. The wedding was good; Jane flew in from Oz; everything was delightful. Then I heard on the news that Margot Fonteyn had died. I phoned Rudolf, and he confirmed the facts, and that was all he had to say about it. He told me to buy a book he wanted, collect some music he'd ordered and meet him in a couple of weeks. End of call. Rudolf's grief was intense but brief. There was work to be done.

9

The Dakota Again
'Nev mind dat'

Late February 1991. Manhattan was very cold. The apartment in the Dakota was very, very hot.

We were back in the old routine, which began each day just before Rudolf awoke and whistled for tea, and didn't end until he went to bed at night. Our first exchange never varied. I said, 'How are you?'

'Alive.'

He croaked the word. His throat was congested when he woke up. On a good day he looked a bit groggy but he got out of bed, stretched, winced, shuffled around the room, drank his tea. It was black and stiff with sugar and laced with lemon juice. Without tea, Nureyev was nothing and nowhere. A little humour did him good, too. Not a joke, not a wisecrack – that would be too demanding. Just a few lighthearted words to make him smile.

That was on a good day. There were other days, mornings when his mind was too dazed and his body too weary to come fully to life. His voice was weak. He had just enough strength to ask for a massage. A good massage knocked his muscles back to life, and his mind followed. Massaging Nureyev had become a daily duty for me on St Barts, where professional masseurs didn't exist. The task was nothing like a relaxing rub-down at a health farm. Dance was pain, and massage was medicine. Nureyev didn't want to be soothed. He wanted to be hammered back into working shape. He wanted a very powerful massage, very deep in the muscles. My hands are not especially big or strong, and I never massaged hard enough for him; but then, neither did the professionals.

He lay face down, and I worked on his feet, calves and thighs. At first, I stopped at the top of his thighs, either from prudence or from prudery. Probably a bit of both. 'Higher!' he said. I was quitting at the very spot where a dancer's leg is made to work the hardest: where the thigh joins the buttock.

'Well. . . .'

'Higher! It won't *bite*.'

He was right, as usual. I massaged the buttocks right down to their link with the thighs, and I massaged hard enough to leave bruises on the average man. The only thing he noticed was that I didn't massage hard enough; I wasn't reaching the pain. The man had muscles like an Olympic skier.

Sometimes he wanted a head massage. The idea is to try to compress the scalp with your fingers, without dragging or scraping at the hair. You keep squeezing the scalp and moving it. It's a tricky act and I never got it quite right.

The final piece of massage was a cure for Rudolf's headaches. I trimmed my thumbnails. He sat in an upright chair, I stood behind him and pressed the tips of my thumbs into the hollow at the top of his neck and the base of his skull. He called this spot 'the ass-hole of the brain'. I leaned and pushed. He said, 'Harder, harder. More.' I'm six-one,

185 pounds. It frightened me, because I was concentrating all my strength and upper body weight on this small, shallow part of his head. 'Harder, harder. ' He called that a good head-scrunch. And his headache disappeared.

As soon as he was revived and he'd had breakfast, he was all action. It was a busy time: his *Friends Tour* in the US wasn't yet finished and the British tour was being planned. When things were going well, Rudolf called Robert 'Schlobert' and me 'Blukes' (he took a boyish pleasure in fooling about with names). When things went badly, he was all scowls and Russian curses. One warning signal was his statement *Nev mind dat!* It meant his time was being wasted. One day I made a simple mistake: dialled a wrong phone number. Rudolf blasted my apology: '*Nev mind dat*! Do what I tell you.' I began to explain; he cut me off. 'Too long. Waste too much time.'

That was why he was pleased when the dancers in New York gave him a fax machine as a present. He liked sending faxes. They wasted no time at all. (Of course he could have bought his own fax machine. He could have bought a dozen. Under my bed in the Paris apartment had been large bolts of the most costly silks, which had lain untouched for years. Rudolf had a weakness for rich fabrics. He bought the stuff by the roll. But a fax machine . . . that was in the same luxury category as toenail clippers.) As luck would have it, this fax machine didn't work. So I took it to the shop, which was run by an Arab. A New Yorker who is also an Arab is a volatile combination. When I got back to the apartment, Rudolf said, 'Is it fixed yet?'

'No, they're going to—'

'Why aren't they fixing it?'

'Well, Rudolf, it takes time to—'

'*Nev mind dat*! What's the number?' He dialled it. 'Dis

Rudolf Nureyev. Where my fax machine?'

I could hear the Arab: 'I dunno who the hell Rudolf Nureyev is. If you—'

Rudolf exploded. *'Why don't you fuck yourself, you cunt!'* he screamed. He whacked the phone down hard enough to break it.

I went back to the shop and got the fax machine thrown at me. The Arab said, 'You hadn't come, I'd of chucked it out the goddam window.'

'Sorry about the boss,' I said. 'He gets a bit temperamental.' Somebody else fixed the machine. Rudolf never asked about it. None of his concern.

To an outsider, his behaviour might have looked like the tantrum of a spoiled brat. Nureyev was more complex than that. His outburst was part of a running battle between the artist and the technician; between the man who wants few details and likes risk, and the man who needs maximum data to ensure certainty. Nureyev had been colliding with technicians all his life. When they wasted his time he blew them away with a broadside. That exhausted his ammunition, so he stumbled off to recover, leaving someone like me to sweep up the wreckage.

Once the fax was up and working, Rudolf used it a lot. He usually paid my salary by faxing an order to his bank in New York (although Luigi once handed me a single thousand dollar bill as my month's pay). Rudolf liked faxing the bank because it was cheap and easy and instantaneous: job done, problem solved, forget it. The bank didn't agree. The bank thought Nureyev was a king-size pain in the butt.

He was visiting Milan when I got a message in New York: go to the Madison Avenue branch and transfer $50,000 to such-and-such an account in Europe. (Why he didn't just fax them, he didn't say. He probably felt I wasn't working hard enough. Rudolf suspected everyone of slacking as soon as his back was turned.) Robert Tracy knew the account handler at the bank. 'Be very polite to her, Blue. She goes through hell every time Rudolf wants something done.' He was right. This simple transfer turned into a major headache, because of Rudolf's slap-happy methods. For a start, he hadn't authorized me to act for him: that was the sort of petty detail he couldn't be bothered with.

Eventually the account handler got it sorted out. I knew she took care of funds for a lot of the rich and famous. I asked, 'How does Rudolf's money-handling compare with the others?'

Before she could stop herself, she said, 'It's the worst.'

When it came to dealing with banks, Rudolf was a mess. For example, he'd describe me in his financial instructions as 'Blue Robinson' – a name the banks didn't, and couldn't, recognize. He spoke to them in his urgent, abbreviated English. It was good for briefing dancers but not much help to an account handler who needed full instructions. Rudolf couldn't give full instructions. He'd choke on the words.

The *Nureyev and Friends* tour was still working its way up the eastern states of America. Between cities, Nureyev would spend a few days at the Dakota. Sometimes he went to the cinema with Robert and me. Nothing highbrow: the sort of movie he enjoyed was one about black gang warfare in New York, especially the scenes where young punks begged for their lives before being rubbed out by ruthless hoods; Rudolf found them very funny. Next night the apartment might be full of people who were so in awe of Rudolf that they didn't know whether to sit or stand, and weren't at all sure what to say. It was a constant reminder of his greatness in the eyes of the dance world.

When he took a taxi, Rudolf couldn't tolerate waiting ten seconds. Preparing to go by plane, he could waste hours, sometimes days.

We were on St Barts when he suddenly decided to fly to Paris again. When? He couldn't say. Soon, very soon. Today or tomorrow. How? He didn't know. There are various routes: via Miami, or via New York, or via God knows where else. OK, he said, book them. Book them all.

Four of us were organizing this flight – each working in isolation. Rudolf told Robert Tracy to do it, *and* me, *and* his travel agent in New York, *and* Luigi Pignotti in Milan. Luigi rang me. 'You don't know what trouble this causes me,' he said. 'You should do your job.' I explained what was going on. Luigi gave a long, weary sigh. He hung up and began calling airlines.

Four people were working independently of each other, booking different flights on different airlines through different routes at different times. Rudolf would look at the list and reject them all. The reason was: he really didn't want to fly. We'd try again, until eventually he bit the bullet and chose a flight. It sounds absurd. It was absurd; but he was the boss, and if he told us to jump, we jumped.

Meanwhile a lot of bookings had been made. This is 'blanket-booking' and it happened all the time. Rudolf might have to fly New York–Paris but he wouldn't know exactly when. We'd book a mid-morning flight in my name, a lunchtime flight in Robert's name, a late-afternoon flight under Pignotti and an evening flight under Wallace Potts. We'd pick up our tickets at the airport. If the airline people said, 'No, it's booked under Pignotti,' we'd say, 'Well, that's our agent.' There was never any hassle. As soon as they saw Nureyev, we were just eased through.

Blanket-booking meant the airline got stuck with a lot of no-shows. That was too bad. If we had time to cancel, we cancelled. Often we were moving so fast – bags packed and everything – there was no time to cancel. Rudolf never lost any sleep over it. And the airline never complained.

If we had to fly he liked Concorde, provided someone else was paying. Andrew Grossman was skilled at persuading ballet companies to fly Rudolf by Concorde. But even Concorde was just an aeroplane: just an object of terror.

We were at the Dakota. Rudolf was booked on Concorde. Take-off was 11 a.m. from Kennedy airport. At 10.15 he was still in bed. To allow less than forty-five minutes to get from midtown Manhattan to Kennedy is to gamble recklessly with snarled traffic and roadworks and possible hold-ups at the bridge or the tunnel. At last Rudolf got out of bed. I had packed. He pulled the stuff out and threw it on the floor. This was the St Barts experience all over again. I repacked. 'Not like that, not like that!' he said. He was so nervous he didn't know what he was saying. By now it was 10.30. I picked up the bag. 'Not like that!' he said. Robert was on the phone to Air France, pleading: *Hold the flight, he's coming.*

Columbia Artists had a limo waiting. We were crossing Manhattan when Rudolf said, 'Don't say anything. I forgot to pack passport.' Neither of us spoke for the rest of the journey. The driver worked a small miracle and got us to Kennedy just before eleven. We raced through the terminal and jumped into the elevator for the Concorde departure lounge. As we went up Rudolf said, 'Get me music score from bag.' It was bang in the middle. As I was fishing it out, he said accusingly, 'You nearly made me miss my flight.' He wasn't rational: wanting the score was a way of avoiding thinking about flying, just as his accusation was a disguised wish, like the 'forgotten' passport. (Being Nureyev, he didn't really need a passport.)

Ironically, there was then a brief delay. We stood in silence in the departure lounge. For added tension, Madonna and her entourage happened to be there too. She and Rudolf glowered at each other. Soon the flight was called and they all went out.

I found a seat and relaxed and thought: *The man's a genius but . . . maybe I should quit now, because it's probably not going to get any easier.* I didn't quit, and the job didn't get any easier. But my problems were as nothing compared with his.

When he wasn't in Paris, or on tour performing with *Nureyev and Friends*, Rudolf sometimes threw a dinner party at the Dakota. That meant ten or twelve guests, with a Russian lady brought in to cook, and Robert and me serving. Mainly the guests were dancers or choreographers, and the talk was gossip about the dance world; so Rudolf felt at ease and cheerful. At one dinner party, a hot piece of glass fell from a chandelier into a woman's soup; amazingly, she didn't notice it until she tried to eat it. (This sounds incredible but I saw it happen.) Rudolf found it hilarious. Next day, and for days afterward, just the memory of it was enough to make him burst into laughter. He had a very schoolyard sense of humour. Sometimes barnyard was a better word.

But there wasn't a great deal of laughter on the night that a young male dancer was one of the guests. He looked very ill; his skin was plastered with scabs. At first glance it was almost as if his face was falling off. Everyone worked hard to make the evening a success, but when the guests had gone Rudolf was unusually thoughtful. His voice was quiet when he asked Robert if that was AIDS. Robert just nodded. The silence was very gloomy indeed.

In 1991, so much was feared and so little was known. The

threat of AIDS hung like a giant thundercloud that might burst catastrophically . . . or it might drift away. By now it was evident to me that the blue-and-white-striped pills were AZT. There was no escaping their importance (AZT was in the news a lot) and Rudolf's continued carelessness about taking them simply meant that the rest of us had to pay more attention. It was a situation that made Robert miserable. He was being torn apart by his emotions.

He desperately wanted Rudolf to be well, but at the same time he was infuriated by Rudolf's reckless attitude. His bitterness was obvious when he told me, 'At least Rudolf can afford the pills. There are so many people who can't.' That was all he had to say. Next day, just to be sure that nobody was under any misunderstanding, I asked Robert why Rudolf was taking them. 'Because he's HIV positive,' Robert said. End of discussion once more. No doubt Robert had lost a lot of friends already, and he was entitled to feel nervous about his own future. During those weeks at the Dakota he grew noticeably edgier. When Rudolf left New York, Robert sometimes became so upset that I had to go out and leave him alone in the apartment. He was upset at Rudolf, not at me; and I knew there was nothing I could say or do to help him. He didn't want to hear from me. He wanted to hear from Rudolf, and Rudolf wasn't interested in him any longer.

And yet it was obvious to us both that Rudolf had an insatiable sexual interest in everybody and everything. Sex was always on his mind. For instance, if he wanted an electrical item to work, he couldn't say, 'Plug it in.' He had to say, 'Put the dick in the cunt.' Everything reminded him of sex: the shape of vegetables in the market, a couple walking the street, an electrical socket. I never saw him with a sexual partner (there were spells, of course, when I was elsewhere) but the idea of sex was something he could never let go.

This obsession, without any apparent sexual outlet, puzzled Robert. 'Maybe it's due to wanking,' he said to me. 'He certainly wanks enough.' That, of course, was no consolation to Robert.

And all the time, memories of Nureyev's genius lay around. His bedroom was like an archive of greatness that nobody had bothered to dust.

They did things on the grand scale when they built the Dakota. The bedroom had walk-in cupboards twelve feet high, with ladders to reach the top. The upper sections contained racks and racks of dance clothes from the sixties and seventies. Down below were angled shoe-shelves, row upon row, packed with his old dance shoes. I picked out a pair. The leather was baked crisp by the heat; they were no use. We needed the space. 'What shall we do with these, Rudolf?'

'Oh . . . don't do anything with them.' He took them from me. 'These were great shoes. I think I did Donkey Shot in those.' (All dancers pronounce *Don Quixote* like that.) He gave them back, I put them in their place. Those shoes were the diary he never kept.

Elsewhere in his bedroom there was a lot of junk: bits of old cameras, broken radios, watches that would never run again, ancient audio cassettes, nothing of any sentimental value. He threw none of it away, just shoved it out of sight until there were big drawers crammed with junk. Scattered about the place was the expensive junk – gifts that he'd received, with huge applause, from grateful ballet companies or rich admirers: chunks of crystal with his name carved; lumps of silver engraved *Love to Rudolf*. There were even some big fossils. Everything was dusty. He didn't want me to clean the room, but once in a while he'd notice the dust, and he'd suggest, uncertainly, 'Can you dust here?

Needs a bit of . . . Can you dust the keys of harpsichord?'

Apart from the lavish furnishings and works of art, Nureyev owned nothing worth taking to a pawnshop except a heavy gold Cartier wristwatch. That too was a gift. It hung so loosely on his wrist that it easily fell off. He rarely wore it. It lay around the bedroom, making Robert nervous of thieves. In any case, Nureyev couldn't be bothered to look at a watch. He never knew the time; he was always asking us; and immediately he wanted to know the time in Milan. If we were in Italy, he wanted to know the time in New York. It got so we had the answer ready before he asked the question.

End of March 1991, and Rudolf was getting ready to go to Britain for a tour that would start in late April. He would be directing as well as dancing. It looked like a lot of travelling and a lot of work. Then he said, 'I was wondering.'

What he was wondering was whether I could paint his farmhouse, near Leesburg in Virginia. He took the plane east. I took the train south.

It wasn't a farmhouse, except in the sense that the people who built it owned a lot of land all around. It was more like something from *Gone with the Wind*: a tall, handsome, two-storey residence built of the small red bricks that Americans like. At the front was a white portico with white balustrades leading up to it from left and right. The portico protected a creamy-white front door that had been built wide enough to let the womenfolk walk in and out in their crinolines. The next side of the house had an even bigger portico. In front of both sides spread a large lawn, which fell away to a stream and many massive trees. Deer came to drink at the stream. A long driveway led down to the road, which was only a country lane. The house was another of Nureyev's wolves' lairs.

There were a couple of dozen rooms. The window-frames were white. I painted them all, and several other bits too, at a fraction of the cost of a firm of professional house-painters. It took three weeks. Then I caught the train to New York and followed Nureyev to England.

10

Britain

'What sort of shit town is Harrogate?'

'Britain?' Nureyev said gloomily, when we were still in New York. 'The critics will rip me to shreds.'

The opening night of the British tour certainly gave the critics plenty of ammunition to fire at him, and his reputation took a bit of a beating. This was a new experience for the maestro. The tour opened at the Sunderland Empire. Sunderland is a long way from the heart of the dance world, which was just as well. The best thing anyone could say was that the lights weren't bad; on the other hand, there were moments when it might have been better if the lights had failed. The opening night was a flop.

Even before this, the atmosphere backstage had not been the happiest. Jeff Kruger was organizing the tour. He had handled tours before, tours by Pat Boone, and Bill Haley and his Comets. He didn't know a vast amount about Rudolf Nureyev or about ballet. His first words to me were, 'I don't know who you are, I don't know why you're here and I'm not paying you to hang around.' Not a promising start. Next day Kruger told me he'd been informed that Rudolf never used white towels because he thought they were unlucky. It was a trivial mistake, but it wouldn't have been a trivial matter if Rudolf had been dripping wet while Kruger's people ran around looking for green, red or blue towels.

The music was not a trivial mistake. The music was a major blunder.

When he was younger, Nureyev had always said he would never dance to taped music. Someone had persuaded him otherwise, and he'd done it in America, and now he was going to do it in Britain. He'd heard the tapes in New York; presumably they sounded OK. He'd been told, 'If you don't have an orchestra, you can have more money. The tapes will be excellent, and the audience won't know the difference.'

But the audience in the Sunderland Empire certainly knew the difference, and it wasn't just the difference between an orchestra playing *for* the dancers, and dancers performing to a tape. The music was awful. It was painful to hear. Something had gone seriously wrong with the sound system. Sometimes it boomed, sometimes it faded. Even when the volume was right, the tone was wrong. There was distortion everywhere. All night the music sounded bad. No matter how skilful dancers are, they can't dance well to bad music. Not surprisingly, quite a few of the audience wanted their money back. What was surprising, however, was their reason.

Many complained about the sound quality, but the main charge was against Nureyev. To his fans he was a huge disappointment, and the bigger the fan, the greater the disappointment. This was inevitable. They had come to see a dancer who had not existed for many years. Rudolf knew it when he said the critics would savage him. The British organizers had promoted the tour simply as *Rudolf Nureyev*, and not as *Nureyev and Friends*, which was how the US tour had been billed. But Nureyev hadn't toured Britain for years. By presenting himself in this way, he was asking for trouble. His admirers arrived in strength at the Sunderland Empire, filled with vibrant memories of the Nureyev who had leaped higher and spun faster than anyone else. They saw some brilliant, spectacular dancing that night, but not from Rudolf.

He'd just passed fifty-three. The leaping and spinning were done superbly well by the other principal dancers, especially Charles Jude and Evelyn Desutter. Rudolf, by contrast, danced 'The Lesson' and 'The Moor's Pavanne' – excellent, artful pieces in their way, but not athletic. They were walking dances. He used them to close the first half and the second, which meant the final curtain went down on a sense of anticlimax. People left feeling that their golden memories had been somehow tarnished, and many wished they'd stayed at home.

From Sunderland the tour moved to Edinburgh. Kruger's people got the music right, and the show was given a fairly warm reception. The Edinburgh audience had probably read the reviews from Sunderland and knew what not to expect of Rudolf. Then he collapsed.

Food poisoning is one of those afflictions, like gout or jaundice or mumps, that other people don't always take seriously – unless they've suffered from it, in which case they know how bad it can be. What makes food poisoning so dreadful is the suddenness with which it strikes. Rudolf and Luigi and I had eaten at a fish restaurant. We returned to the hotel, and went up to Rudolf's room. One minute he was standing and chatting; the next minute he couldn't

111

stand, his guts were giving him acute pain, he was trying to throw up and failing, and liquid food was dribbling out of his nose. He thought he was dying. So did we, briefly. But Rudolf wasn't completely helpless. He had just enough strength to panic, and in his panic, only one name mattered. 'Call Canesi!' he pleaded. 'Call Canesi!'

Michel Canesi was the only doctor Nureyev then had, and he trusted him absolutely; but Canesi was in Paris, and it was midnight. Luigi and I wanted to get a local doctor. Rudolf wouldn't hear of it. 'Phone Canesi!' he demanded. 'Must talk to him!'

We got Canesi on the line, and he calmed Rudolf down. 'If it's food poisoning, it'll be gone in twenty-four hours, one way or another. You'll either pass it or vomit it.'

Rudolf's eyes were full of fear. At the time, the simple explanation for this seemed to be that his body – this marvellous mechanism that had brought him all the advantages he'd enjoyed in life – had suddenly betrayed him, and left him helpless. Later I knew that this was only part of the story. Rudolf was living his life under the threat of AIDS. Sprawled in that Edinburgh hotel room, he had to face the terrifying possibility that maybe the disease was taking hold. Maybe this was the beginning of the end.

Nureyev was extraordinarily sensitive to any change in his body. When he was in Paris in the sixties (so he told me) he caught a venereal disease. 'I used to fly to Paris from London for sex. God, it was great. The English were too prudish and reserved, but in Paris!' He knew he had VD because he woke up one morning and felt the change within him. Medical tests confirmed this. Rudolf took the news in his stride. He felt sure that he could beat VD just as he had overcome all the other injuries and illnesses in his career. It was just a matter of sweating it out. Work cures all.

In Edinburgh, that belief was severely tested. In the

event, Canesi's diagnosis was right, and Rudolf's body was still amazingly resilient. It disposed of the food poisoning. Next night he was on stage again, dancing.

During a rehearsal in Edinburgh, Rudolf was standing in the wings, shouting, 'Moooskva! Moooskva!' He was shouting at André Fedatov, who was dancing the leading role in *Le Corsaire*. It calls for some high-speed and spectacular action. In his early years, Rudolf had shown the West how to dance it. Now Fedatov was whirling around the stage and Rudolf was telling him, 'Moooskva!'

A dancer translated for me. 'Moooskva is Moscow. He means, "Go to Moscow!" Distance! Travel! Stretch! Extend yourself!'

Fedatov could hear Rudolf, but he wasn't doing enough to satisfy him. Eventually Rudolf just said, '*Pizdat*,' a very insulting word in Russian. Later he explained why he was disappointed. 'I told him – make distance. To dance in small circles is more difficult. You dance around yourself. Dancer must extend dance area. Must *stretch*, and look, and hang. Not just twirl, hope miracle will happen. Won't happen.'

Much later, I found a video of Nureyev dancing *Le Corsaire*. The speed and passion and footwork are staggering. He watched it without excitement. 'Yes, that was good,' he said. Then we watched his solo from Act III of *Sleeping Beauty* – around and around a crowded stage, endlessly bounding and spinning, faster and faster. This interested him. 'Halfway through that,' he said, 'when I was going around the houses, I could hear audience screaming. So I extended and stretched. And then stopped.' We watched him stop. After a whirlwind of dance, his mouth is closed and he is breathing through his nose.

But the rest of the video bored him. It was all past, all forgettable. What concerned him was the here and now.

113

Fedatov was one of several foreign dancers he had invited to join his tour because he had faith in their talent. He wanted to improve that talent. He told Fedatov, 'Do the whole piece, before the performance. ' That meant, in the warm-up, Fedatov should do more than walk through his principal steps; he should actually dance them. He would end up gasping and sweating. But his mind would be sharply focused, and his muscles would know their way, and his lungs would be fired up. 'You have to stretch the lungs,' Rudolf said. Fedatov's lungs remained unstretched. 'The shit-boy wouldn't do it,' Rudolf said. Zoltan Solymosi, on the other hand, always made the extra effort. Solymosi wasn't a cautious dancer. He stretched, he went to Moscow, and he electrified the audience. Rudolf approved.

After Edinburgh, London. The tour went into one of the smaller performance spaces at Wembley. Being London, there were a lot of Rudolf's friends in the audience. A German impresario was travelling with us, and at the final curtain he and Luigi stood in the wings, just out of sight, and shouted *bravo!* That nudged the audience, and their *bravos* came thick and fast.

So Rudolf's dressing-room was full of congratulations from such as Maude Gosling and the designer Tessa Kennedy and Irek Mukhamedov. He'd recently left the Bolshoi to join the Royal Ballet; like Rudolf, he was a superb and passionate dancer. I heard Rudolf tell him, 'Follow your own nose. That's what I did. Don't get trapped.' Later, during the tour, Rudolf asked him to join his company and Mukhamedov repeated Rudolf's advice back to him and declined the offer.

There was little rest on tour: travel, rehearsal and performance took up most of the day. One period that permitted time for quiet was when Rudolf sat in his dressing-room and put on his make-up. Luigi and I said very little. We sat and watched him.

He wanted us there, but sometimes it was hard to feel we were not intruding on his privacy. We were watching a man looking at a large mirror, studying the reflection of his life in his face. The face was ageing, the life was fading. What was he thinking about? The piece he was about to dance? The roles he could no longer dance? The famous stages he had danced them on? The boyish good looks that had been an international symbol of the sixties and seventies?

He would push his hair back. 'I had such beautiful hair.' That was said softly. We all knew his hair was getting thin. After a long while, just staring and thinking, he'd pinch his cheeks. 'What d'you think, Shluigi? Should I have a cheek job? Couple of tucks? Here, and here? Like Hollywood?' They were tentative questions, meant to make us laugh. 'Do you think I'd look better, Blooksh? Would it improve me?' He would look at his face from different angles. 'Perhaps not.'

When he began making-up, he was still thoughtful and unhurried. 'What sort of shit town is Harrogate?' he would enquire.

'Oh, it's supposed to be quite nice, Rudolf.'

It wasn't a serious question; just words. Every place got the same treatment. 'Where is this shit town Bournemouth?' . . . 'How big is this shit town Nottingham?'

The truth was that the tour covered sixteen venues in twenty-one days, and very few of them were big. The Cambridge Corn Exchange and Portsmouth Guildhall were modest places for a man of his reputation. That's how he wanted it. Get egg on your face at the Malvern Festival Theatre and you can wipe it off and move on. Do the same at the London Coliseum and your reputation suffers every-where. Nureyev needed to hang on to his reputation; he planned to return as a conductor. He hated it when the Press called this his 'farewell tour'.

But in that case, why did he do the damn tour at all?

He explained himself by accident. I happened to mention that the first ballet I ever saw was in Nepal. The Bolshoi's second company, on an Asian tour, was dancing on a small, dirty, uneven stage in a rickety stadium that was half-empty. The audience was made up of Nepalese men smoking fat cheroots and Nepalese women who gossiped while they nursed their babies. Many of the babies were crying. 'Must have been awful for the dancers ' I said.

'Eediott!' Rudolf said. '*Those* are the people to dance to. They came, brought family, enjoyed dance. That's what touring company is about. Better than dance to rich society types, don't give a damn, can't remember name of performance after. Take dance to people in provinces.'

'Even if the stage is bad?'

'Doesn't matter. Get out, do it. Show dance to people.'

And show people to dancers. Rudolf used the British tour to introduce and train new and talented dancers. Some came from Russia; it was a big break for them, and good money because it was in sterling. One night, the showbiz cliché actually happened: a principal dancer got hurt, the youngest dancer took her place and took her chance and was a stunning success. That was heaven for her and good for Rudolf. All he was interested in was dance. Dance was his life. He was dead off-stage.

During the performance, he left his dressing-room as late as possible. It was my job to give him an accurate countdown, which meant knowing the ballet back to front. A typical sequence went like this:

'Rudolf, the girls have just come off, two acts before you.'

116

Later, 'Girls have come on, an act before you.' Then, 'Rudolf, it's halfway through the act before you.' At which he'd say, 'Halfway? Right, I'll walk up. . . .' And we'd reach the wings in nice time, but not so soon that he'd be hanging about in the draughts.

One night, on the British tour, he was studying a score: Mozart's 40th Symphony. Hot stuff.

'Two acts before you, Rudolf.' He raised a hand. The other hand was beating time: *tum-ti-tum-ti-tum*.

'An act before you.' Hand raised. *Tum-ti-tum*.

'They've finished the act before you, so you're on in two minutes.' Hand raised. *Tum-ti-tum*.

Very soon, the curtain was closed. The dancers formed a semicircle on stage, ready for 'The Moor's Pavanne'.

'Rudolf!'

'What? What?'

'They're on stage! I've been telling you!'

'*What*? Why didn't you tell me?'

His costume for 'The Moor's Pavanne' was red tights, which he was wearing, and a red tailcoat, which he wasn't. The coat had to be hooked and buttoned all the way up the front. A lot of buttons. A hell of a lot of buttons. He put on the coat and ran and I ran with him, buttoning as we ran. When we reached the wings, the curtains had already been closed too long, and his coat still wasn't buttoned. The stagehands and lighting guys woke up. At last, some excitement in their dull lives!

Rudolf had an iron-clad rule that I never go on stage during a performance. So I stopped.

'Come on!' he urged, 'Come on!'

We ran on, me desperately stuffing buttons into button-holes. Rudolf linked arms with Charles Jude and Evelyn Desutter. 'Come on, come on! Last one!' The music had started. There were exactly four bars to go. The last button

slipped into place. When those curtains open they acceler-
ate with a whoosh. I turned and ran. The curtains were
chasing me. I leaped into the wings – and got a round of
applause from the blokes. 'Well jumped, mate!' they said.
'You takin' up dancin', are you?'

At the end of the piece I was waiting in the wings with
the towel and the tea. 'Good performance?'

'Oh, not bad.' He'd forgotten everything. The audience
hadn't noticed anything odd. That's what comes of being at
the top for thirty years. You take it all in your stride.

Or nearly all.

The how and why of curtain calls is something most
theatre-goers never give a thought to. They probably
assume the star decides if the applause is healthy, gives a
stagehand a nod, and up goes the curtain. It didn't work
like that on the British tour.

We had an American stagehand who'd worked with
Rudolf in the States; he knew the drill; he operated the
curtains quickly and slickly – which is how it should be. An
audience should never be left beating its palms together for
nothing. On this particular evening the audience was
appreciative. The company took their call, then the principal dancers. Rudolf took a call, and returned for a second
call. The applause surged. He stepped back, the curtains
closed, the applause faded. *Then they opened again.* He had
no choice but to come forward. People were leaving their
seats. The applause picked up, in a faltering half-hearted
way. He made his bow, stepped back. Curtains closed. The
applause died. Rudolf looked at the American stagehand.
'Aaaah . . . Shit-boy,' he said.

'I'm really sorry,' the man said.

'It happens,' Rudolf said. 'Shouldn't happen.'

Meanwhile, people going into the street were saying,
'Did you see that? See how Nureyev tried to milk the audi-

ence for more applause?' And there was no way that anyone could tell them it wasn't so.

During the tour, two changes were becoming obvious in Rudolf. One was his increasing fatigue. The other was a turning inwards that amounted almost to indifference to the outside world. The two changes may well have been linked.

Luigi recognized these signs before I did. It was during the British tour that he knew Rudolf had developed full-blown AIDS. Nobody spoke of his condition. (The most that Luigi ever said to me was 'Be careful', but that could have meant anything.) We all took our lead from Rudolf. If he had discussed his health openly, we would have responded; since he was silent, so were we. Whenever an outsider asked me if Rudolf was HIV positive, I always turned the question back: 'Would you like people to discuss your medical condition behind your back?' That ended that.

Rudolf's first waking moments each day often revealed a man barely able to speak. I always asked, 'How are you?' His reply used to be a croak; now he could just manage a whisper: 'Alive.' It was as if the strain and pressure of the tour had exhausted him; and yet he slept as long as he could; often half the day. Massage was essential to revive his body. Good professional masseurs, with experience in the world of sport or dance, were hard to find. When I paid them – £50 or £60 a time – they were always sweating. 'Bloody hell,' one masseur said. 'He's hard work! Never had anything like *that* before.'

The reviews of the tour were patchy and Rudolf wasn't interested in them. He was doing the best he could; he wasn't going to waste his time trying to please people who wanted the impossible; so he closed his mind to the outside

119

world. When he wasn't sleeping or dancing he worked at learning how to conduct. Orchestral scores went everywhere with him. And always he had his rules, learned through bitter experience.

He taught me never to put anything in hotel drawers. Everything had to go on top, where it was visible; otherwise it might get forgotten.

He taught me to focus on what matters. One night, after the performance, as I undressed him, he dropped a towel. I bent to pick it up. He said, quietly, 'Leave towel. I'm getting cold. It's a shit towel. What's a towel worth? Wrap me up before I get a chill.'

He taught me to dry things with a hair-dryer, for speed. A sweaty pair of trousers that he'd been dancing in would dry in minutes with hot air blasting through them.

He taught me to lock the dressing-room door. Without fail. People always *took* from him: autographs, handshakes, smiles, property. Souvenir hunters were a constant menace. They'd steal anything: his scarf, his hat, his dance clothes.

'Trust no one,' he said. 'No-o-o-o-o one.'

'Even me?'

'Especially you.'

But he did trust me; he had no choice. I often carried his long green raincoat, the one with the special button-down inside pocket where he kept his wallet and passport. Every time I picked it up he said, 'Check everything is there. Check pocket is buttoned.' I'd done it a hundred times before, I did it ten times a day. Still . . . one day I might forget. One day it might be someone else, some junior dancer assigned to be his dresser. Rudolf never forgot. Only he knew just how hard-earned that money was.

Nureyev was lonely, and liked it. Perhaps, at this stage in his life, he was happy to be lonely. Certainly there were

A couple of big-deal US photographers arrived on Li Galli for a shoot, which is why Rudolf is wearing this rich robe – it matched the antique Spanish tiles on most of his walls. Their pictures made him look like an eastern potentate

Rudolf looking like a medieval monarch. The tiles on the walls and floor merge into the fabric which has been thrown over the coach, which in turn merges into the kaftan-style gown he is wearing. He looks truly regal - and slightly absurd!

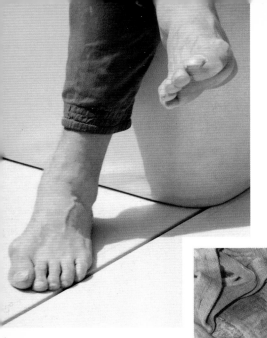

The multi-million-dollar feet. Picture taken when we went by boat from Li Galli to Capri, for dinner. Gore Vidal, a near neighbour, reckoned that 'for a dancer' the feet weren't in bad shape: 'not too misshapen, no hammertoes'

Rudolf bought this Greek statue for $50,000. He preferred the back to the front. He used to lie on a couch, while we slowly rotated the statue until he got a perfect view of the cheeks

Rudolf Nureyev's practice shoes – one of many pairs. I took this shot just before I mended the toes. Certain pairs were his favourites; he hated to see them wear out

Rudolf rehearses an outdoor co trapped her thumb in a folding c can be principal?' A frozen vodk Rud

Chichi on Li Galli, sheltering beneath some of Nureyev's costly fabrics. Rudolf called him 'Chichikoff' and held intimate, slanderous conversations with him. Chichi, always the soul of courtesy, never interrupted

The dining room at Nureyev's Manhattan apartment. Guests are about to enter, so the candles have just been lit. Rudolf left it late, to save money. One guest that night was suffering advanced AIDS; another tried to eat a piece of hot glass that fell from a chandelier into her soup. A memorable evening

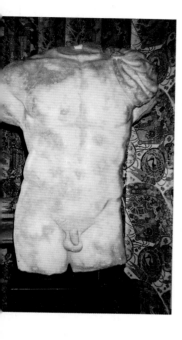

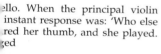

...ello. When the principal violin ...instant response was: 'Who else ...red her thumb, and she played. ...;ed

Rehearsing *L'après-midi d'un faune* in an outdoor arena near Amalfi. On stage Rudolf succeeded in looking wafer-thin – almost two-dimensional. He told me he'd studied film of Nijinski, especially the hands, to help master this role. The Italian organizer had recently lost her son in a car crash. Rudolf sympathized and said, 'Work conquers all,' a maxim he applied to himself. It worked, up to a point

The dining-room in Paris with some examples of Nureyev's taste in paintings of muscular male nudes. The table is still covered with his mail. I dealt with it. He never read letters

Nureyev was a highly talented collector, but sometimes I felt he never knew when to stop. The Paris apartment piled richness upon richness. It was a feast for the eye and a bitch to dust

Nureyev's Paris apartment. No shortage of works of art, and this wasn't even a room – more a sort of passage leading to his bedroom, which is just visible through the door

occasions when he seemed glad to escape from others; he was far more at ease in his own company. He could even, it seemed, do without sex. Except once.

The tour had reached the Midlands. The performance was over, it was late, the company was going back to the hotel. Rudolf lingered, and let the others go into the lobby first. This was strange. I waited beside him. He said he was going for a walk. That was more than strange; it was unprecedented. The last thing he needed was exercise. He wandered into the night, and turned to walk behind the hotel. There was only one explanation: he was looking for a man. After a while he reappeared at the other side of the building, ambling along, peering into the shadows. Eventually, and very slowly, we drifted back into the warmth of the hotel. He was neither depressed nor uncomfortable; just thoughtful. It was a sad little episode.

When Nureyev wasn't all-conquering he could appear to be very susceptible indeed. During the British tour he was never brought lower – food poisoning apart – than on the night he couldn't get some chicken legs.

We were in a hotel in Bournemouth, Rudolf and Luigi and me. He was tired and hungry. He wanted to eat something light and go to bed. Chicken, salad, a baked potato. When he ate chicken he ate only the legs. He said chicken legs helped dancers dance.

I called the kitchen, placed the order, told them to send it up. Time passed. He got hungrier. 'I don't know,' he said. 'I'm really very hungry.' He was restless, weary, bored with the whole business. 'I'm getting *past* hunger. Maybe I'll just . . . just go to bed.'

Luigi phoned the kitchen: 'Can you hurry up the chicken legs?' They said yes. They lied. More time passed. No chicken legs arrived. Then a waiter delivered a tray, and went away. I lifted the warming cover from the plate, and

121

there lay a steak. It was huge, gross. It overlapped the plate at both ends. Rudolf, dead-beat as he was, grabbed it, wrenched open the door, and had his arm back to hurl it at the waiter when we cried out, 'No!' Rudolf slumped. We took it from his hands.

He was filled with despair. If he knew how to weep, he would have wept. 'I just want chicken legs! Is it too difficult to get. . . .'

'We'll get chicken legs.'

Rudolf pointed at me. 'You – Go down to kitchen. Stand over chef. Make him cook chicken legs. And a potato. Go.'

I went. The chef cooked. Rudolf ate. Luigi and I had the steak.

If we hadn't been there, and the steak had gone flying down the corridor, there would have been meat and gravy everywhere and reports in the gossip columns about a Nureyev tantrum. That would have been nothing new: he was supposed to be a fiery Tartar. What was new was his weariness, and his despair. In Cleveland, Ohio, at the gala reception where no one offered him food, he soon bounced back to life after he'd had something to eat. On St Barts, when he thought my taking a shower would delay his dinner, he had the strength to be furious. Now, four months later, a permanent fatigue was eating into his appearance, and also into his ability to cope with a crisis over chicken legs.

But— Rudolf was nothing if not buoyant. The British tour ended, at Brighton, on 17 May 1991. Next day we flew to Verona, where he had five days to learn a new ballet, and where he kicked a young black dancer so hard that he (the dancer) went to hospital for three days and sued Nureyev for one and a half million dollars. There was life in those old legs yet.

11

Verona

'A quick, short kick on the backside'

The ballet that Nureyev went to Verona to learn was *Death in Venice*.

With hindsight, there is something chilling about this event. *Death in Venice* is the story of a middle-aged man, Aschenbach, besotted by a beautiful youth whom he sees on the beach. It's a hopeless, painful passion, and over it all hangs the threat of death: plague is closing in on Venice. Rudolf danced the part of Aschenbach. The parallels with his own life were everywhere in the story. Indeed, reality was more tragic than fiction, because in life Rudolf could never find the golden boy who appeared before Aschenbach; and Rudolf did not wander innocently into a plague city: he carried his own private plague with him.

None of this showed on the surface. He was coming straight off the British tour, and he had only five days to learn the ballet, so he had to dig deep into his reserves. But dance was like a blood transfusion for him. In Verona,

123

when he was on-stage he came to life. Off-stage, he was almost sleep-walking. When he awoke, when he tried to put his feet on the floor and felt the pain in his muscles, he groaned, 'Ah . . . shit.' He hobbled around like a cripple. Then he took a bath, very hot, hotter than I could stand, so hot that it left him bright red. I scrubbed his back.

This was a form of massage; I used a sisal-string glove with soap on it. He demanded to be scrubbed very hard. I never wore out his back, but the day came when I wore out the palm of the glove. I switched the glove from my right to my left hand, so that the back of the glove became the palm, which gave me a fresh surface to scrub with.

'I had to do that,' he said. 'I damaged right foot. Used to lead with right leg, now had to train left leg to lead. Give right leg a rest. Survived as dancer. Learned to dance left *and* right, so on bad nights I could perform.'

One of the first things Rudolf did when he went into the theatre at Verona – or into any theatre – was to walk the stage, every square foot of it. To the audience, a stage is a stage. To any good dancer, a stage is a minefield. Rudolf demonstrated this. Some boards are good and some are not. The bad boards are stiff, the good boards springy. 'Dance on bad board, you don't get any air. Dance on good board, you get extra six inches.' So he found out the geography of the stage and shifted his performance accordingly. He also had a keen eye for dust.

There is a famous photograph of Rudolf snatching the broom from the man who is sweeping the stage, while Margot Fonteyn stands in the background, laughing. He snatched many brooms, in many different theatres. He did it because the man whose job it was to sweep the stage always began in the wings and worked his way across the stage to the opposite wings. 'Don't do that, eediott!' Rudolf would shout. 'Start in *middle* of stage, sweep *left*, go *back* to middle, and sweep *right!*'

The man would halt, looking thoroughly baffled. 'What?' This would waste two seconds, maybe three – long enough to infuriate Rudolf.

'Look what you're doing! You're pushing dust all across stage! Eediott!' By starting in the wings, the man was brushing dust *onto* the stage. He was making the problem worse.

He soon forgot. Next day he would do it again, and Rudolf would blast him again. And again. Rudolf had the greater stamina. He always won. As he said, 'It's not *his* career. It's *my* career. ' And he explained why dust is so dangerous. 'Dust is worst thing you can land on. You land on edge of foot, and there is dust – you slip and break something.' That fine strip of leather carries all the dancer's weight, and carries it at high speed. If it hits a layer of dust there is no grip. The foot skids.

Sweeping the stage calls for two wide brooms. The second has a rag beneath it to absorb the dust. At one theatre, Rudolf lost all patience with the stage sweeper. 'Aaaah!' he snorted. He took charge of the brooms. 'Luigi! You take one. Blue! You take one.' We swept. He supervised.

One reason why so much stage-sweeping takes place is the rate at which things fall off. Dancers whirl, and baubles and spangles and feathers and buttons go flying. This debris could cause injuries. So could other dancers.

'Foof! They don't care!' Rudolf said. 'When you're holding their hand, and spinning them, their foot comes out and kicks you in balls. And girls' nails, sharp nails, catch you on chin. Dance is dangerous! You got really to be careful. They swing arm in wrong place, wrong time, they *whack* you!

They don't care. Happened to me. Often. Dancer spins fast, makes mistake, fingernail gets ripped off! Blood everywhere.'

Such are the occupational hazards of ballet. But they had nothing to do with the infamous boot in the backside that got Nureyev splashed all over the delighted tabloids. That, according to him, was self-defence.

To learn the leading role in *Death in Venice*, five days didn't seem much. For Rudolf, it was enough. 'There are no new steps in ballet,' he said. 'I know all steps. It's matter of throwing all together. I understand new routine after ten minutes. After second day, choreographer and I know what's happening.' Rudolf didn't need to be shown everything. He kept saying, 'OK, don't do whole step, I know that. Next?' Soon he was rehearsing the entire ballet. And then I got sent away, and missed the drama.

Rudolf had a tiny island called Li Galli, near Capri.

I flew to Naples, drove south along the coast road, all hairpin bends and stupendous views, to Positano, and took a boat the couple of miles to Li Galli. I cleaned and swept the villa, stocked the kitchen, got ready for him. He arrived the day after *Death in Venice* closed, very tired, very glad to be where nobody could bother him and he could sleep all he liked. For the first time in a month he looked relaxed.

I served dinner. We always dined together. What he ate, I ate. 'How did the performance go, Rudolf?'

'Good.' (I learned later it was a triumph.) He took a sip of wine. 'Oh ... I kicked somebody. There is big drama. Anyway ... Pass salad.'

By now, even I knew that there is nothing very extraordinary about a kick in a ballet company. Dancers fight. They punch, they throw things, they even bite: not often, but it happens. Nureyev was no exception. His temper was hotter than most, and in the course of a long, intensive career he took a swing at more than one colleague. Some of them might even have asked for it. Rudolf had nothing more to say about the kick at Verona. I forgot it.

A couple of weeks later the faxes began flying and the big drama turned into high Italian melodrama with overtones of low farce. That, of course, was not how the lawyers saw it; and because Rudolf couldn't write he had to dictate to me his version of events.

It all happened during rehearsal, and it involved a young black male dancer called Almeida. (The fact of his being black is worth mentioning only because it gave the tabloids another angle to work on.) In one scene, Almeida held Rudolf's raised arms while Rudolf performed a series of twisting movements; then Almeida brought Rudolf's arms down to his sides. It was a routine move. It called for no special emphasis. Almeida, according to Rudolf, gave it so much emphasis that it hurt. He didn't bring the arms down; he *slammed* them down. 'He looked excited,' Rudolf told me. 'His eyes were not natural. Look of madness.'

Rudolf complained to Almeida and he complained to the director, Carboni, and at the next rehearsal Almeida did it again, only worse.

'Almeida repeated the same actions, pulling my hands down with great force and looking into my eyes to make sure I received the pain.' What's more, Almeida had long fingernails and 'he was plunging them into my flesh. . . .' This time Rudolf complained to the ballet master, who assured him it wouldn't happen again and Almeida's nails would be cut. But it did, and they weren't. Rudolf complained to the assistant director. He was told not to worry; it was all sorted out.

By now they were into dress rehearsals. Almeida, Rudolf

said, seemed to be 'more out of control than ever. He twisted my hands and arms and pulled them down with a forceful, violent snap – scratching me below the eye with his fingernails in the process – and staring me full in the face. So the inevitable thing had to happen.'

As Rudolf described it, 'I was standing face-to-face with him, and he received a quick, short kick on the backside.' Rudolf, of course, was wearing dance shoes, which weigh only a couple of ounces. 'It could not have caused him any damage or pain, as I was standing in front of him, and his backside is ample.'

The Press reported that Almeida went to hospital and stayed there for three days 'for observation'. His lawyers sued Rudolf for a million and a half dollars. Rudolf dictated to me a long fax, which I sent to his lawyer in Milan, laying out the facts. As far as I know that's where the matter ended. Rudolf never spoke of it again.

All the same . . . it was an odd business. Rudolf was only dancing in *Death in Venice*, not directing. He wasn't running the show, as he had been at La Scala, where he fired (and re-hired) a dissident ballerina on the spot. He couldn't fire Almeida. But his behaviour was not what you'd expect of Nureyev. His complaints all failed but he went on complaining, wasting his time. The old Nureyev would have complained *once*, and if that failed he would have hit the roof and gone through it and landed in St Barts.

By his own standards, his handling of the Almeida affair was feeble. He was tired: too tired to put up a real fight. Those who knew him well could see that he was losing weight; it seemed that his spirit was beginning to shrink too.

12

Li Galli

'Foof! Too slow'

Nureyev's island was a chunk of rugged rock in the Mediterranean. It was more of an islet than an island: it covered a space about the size of two football pitches. Most of that was steep cliffs. The biggest flat space – a patio next to his house – was about the size of a tennis court. It was typical of Rudolf that he rode his motorbike round and round this space, very badly and without a helmet. He always looked as if he was about to fall off but he never did.

Of all his wolves' lairs, Li Galli was by far the least accessible. It had a very tiny jetty and a helipad. Rudolf relished the idea of choppering to and from his island while the seas crashed against it and no boat could land; that was one reason why he bought the place. What he hadn't appreciated was that if the weather was too rough for a boat then it would also be too gusty for a helicopter. The pad was never used. He didn't care. He loved big seas; the sight of huge waves pounding on rock excited him. If we got trapped on the mainland, he would announce, 'The weather has turned us back.' The sea versus Nureyev! Worthy opponents.

But during the first half of that summer we rarely left Li Galli. Rudolf became virtually a recluse. Whether or not this was a response to the increasing grip of AIDS is impossible to say, but as the year went by he became massively indifferent to anything that didn't come out of his own head. He paid no attention to what Robert or Luigi or his bank suggested. Often he wasn't interested in people; the further he distanced himself from them, the better. Li Galli was about as remote as he could get and still have someone to cook his scrambled eggs. (Without that someone, he would have starved.) So Rudolf had the comfort of solitude plus the reassurance that I was always on hand. I couldn't leave. We had no boat.

I am not a recluse. After a few weeks the novelty of isolation wore off: I called the place Alcatraz. But that was my fault; I should have paid more attention to what Rudolf had said. Soon after we moved to Li Galli, he strolled up to me and asked, 'How long can you live here?' It was an unexpected question, and not an easy one. 'Too late!' he said. 'You take too long to answer! Have to be direct.' My mind didn't work like that, I said. 'Foof! Too *slow.*' And he strolled on. Rudolf was no fool. He probably suspected that I would go stir-crazy on a large rock with no other company except mosquitoes hungry for blood. (We slept under mosquito nets.) He was right. Nobody could be locked up with Nureyev for long without banging on the walls.

Approached by boat, the island looks gaunt and forbidding: just a jagged rock rising vertically from the sea. It turned out to be surprisingly comfortable, if limited. You could walk from end to end, slowly, in seven minutes. You couldn't walk from side to side without falling down a cliff.

In Italian, Li Galli means 'cock' as in male hen. It looked nothing like a cock or any kind of poultry. Seen from the air it somewhat resembled a very deformed whale. The whale's head was the highest point; below that it narrowed at the neck and widened to make a long, irregular body. This narrowed again and then branched out in steep cliffs that looked vaguely like a whale's tail. This tail formed a little bay where it was possible to swim.

The seven-minute walk used a path flanked with trees that went along the spine of the island, past Rudolf's house in the middle, up to the Tower at the top end. Below the Tower on one side was the little jetty; on the other side were the remains of a small Roman bathing pool. That ends the guided tour of Li Galli. Its most spectacular assets were its splendid views of the distant mainland, or of the even more distant Capri. When the weather closed in, Li Galli's charms dwindled rapidly.

Amazingly, the island came with a resident population. The old man – we never knew his name – lived in a dim cottage halfway down the cliffs, below Rudolf's villa. Even more amazingly, he managed to live a completely separate life; we saw little of him. He survived by fishing, and netting small birds, and drinking a ferocious *grappa*. I tasted it once. It was like anti-freeze.

The first thing you saw when you landed on Li Galli was a big sign: ATTENTI IL CANE. Beware of the dog. This was the old man's pocket-sized black-and-white mongrel, called Chichi. Chichi was about as dangerous as St Francis of Assisi. He had the manners of a saint, too. He never begged. He always came around when dinner was served and watched from a respectful distance. If a piece of food was offered he accepted it courteously. He behaved just the same if a lot of food was offered. Sometimes my cooking slipped its gears and Chichi got a whole bowl of pasta. He ate the lot. Never got any fatter. Rudolf liked Chichi; he called him Chichikoff. He used to put his head close to the dog's and whisper, in a sinister monotone, 'Halitosis . . . Halitosis, Chichikoff. . . .' There was nothing wrong with the dog's breath. Rudolf simply like the sound of certain words, and he would use them whether they were relevant or not. He enjoyed saying 'Mediocrity'. He said it to me sometimes: 'Meeeediocrity. . . .' Maybe he was trying to tell me something. Maybe not. Who could tell?

Léonide Massine had owned Li Galli, and that was another aspect that appealed to Nureyev. In the years between the wars, Massine had been almost as famous a dancer as Nureyev; and Diaghilev – certainly the greatest dance impresario of the century – gave Massine this island; so it had a certain dance pedigree. Rudolf took pleasure in playing the part of Massine's successor. He found an old megaphone. When sightseers used to arrive in boats, Massine had stood on the clifftops and boomed at them, 'Get off my property!' So now Rudolf did the same, for fun. However, if the joke backfired and people scrambled ashore, Rudolf went into a furious Russian sulk and shut himself away until they left.

We had a little Kawasaki jet-ski. I used to drive it around the island and try to negotiate with Neapolitan boat-owners, who had come out to visit the island and then discovered that they couldn't anchor because the water was too deep. My offer was: it's OK to tie up to the rocks but please don't come ashore. Their response was to tie up to the rocks and come ashore. There were parties and picnics, with *bambini* crawling about and plastic wrappings left to litter the place. It drove Rudolf to a state of deep despair. Once, when a woman got off a boat in his dock and began strolling around, he lost all control. He ran down and cursed her and she cursed him back until he was in a frenzy and I had to get between them. She was in her element, whilst he was heading for emotional collapse. I steered him indoors. Next day the local paper ran a story with a big picture of Nureyev over the headline: *Rudolf and his Robusti-Boy*. Robusti-boy means 'thug'. The builders who were working on the island thought that was very funny. Even Rudolf smiled.

Oddly enough, he was not upset by a tourist boat that used to circle the island, while someone delivered a loud-speaker commentary, first in English, then in Italian. This often took place quite early in the morning, so Rudolf could wake up and lie in bed listening to an account of his glorious achievements. He rather enjoyed that.

Massine had built the villa where Rudolf now lived. (I had a small bungalow nearby.) It was a roomy, pleasant affair, with splendid views. The bath was a handsome creation made of copper and standing on four legs. With both bathroom doors open, Rudolf could lie in the bath and see Positano on the mainland and then turn his head and see Capri out to sea. The patio was on one side of the house; on the opposite side, steps led down to a big kitchen, and next to that was a long, high, domed room that lay underneath the house. This was where the builders were working. Rudolf was having it completely tiled, every inch, with tiles he'd found in Turkey and Spain. They were old, handsome and valuable; he was a shrewd collector. The workmen came by boat every day from Monday to Friday, which was very handy: they brought fresh food for us. The only alternative was to phone a Positano restaurant and ask them to send out a boat, and since our phone was the same battered old portable I'd failed to raise when I tried to call Rudolf from the Pacific, communications were not always reliable. Rudolf didn't care. He didn't understand the technology so he kept punching buttons until somebody answered.

The other building on Li Galli was the Tower, a three-storey structure where guests could stay. Massine had added that too, but his builders had used unwashed sand in the cement and the place was crumbling. Massine had brought his family to live on Li Galli and he educated the children in the Tower. Little piles of mildewed textbooks on Russian, German, science, English and geography were still lying around, as well as exercise books filled with the sad scrawl of the very young. There was even a tiny pair of ballet shoes in a cupboard. According to Rudolf, Massine's kids hated the island. There was no escape from it, or from father.

But the Tower had one overwhelming attraction. Massine had installed a dance studio. Not many island hideaways come equipped with somewhere to have a scrape.

Nureyev never read letters. Letters did not interest him; they were of no importance. Anything that was of no importance to Nureyev was of no importance to anyone: that's how his mind worked. And that's why I got no letters either. Friends wrote to me, usually via Luigi, who gave the letters to Rudolf, who forgot about them, or lost them. Probably both. For example, in October 1991 I was unpacking his bag when I came across a birthday card to me from my sister, which she'd sent in May of that year. The card wasn't hidden – just forgotten. Letters didn't matter. What didn't matter didn't exist. Only Nureyev mattered to Nureyev.

Dinner demanded conversation. Cooking the meal wasn't enough; Nureyev wanted entertainment to be provided too. Nothing dangerous: it wasn't wise to challenge his views on anything; but it was always a good idea to have a topic ready when you sat down to eat. One night, when he seemed unusually thoughtful, I asked if he was looking back on his thirty years in the West. 'I'd have to be *really* drunk to do that,' he said.

Instead, he opened up about his life *before* he came to the West. 'When I was six I saw a ballet in Ufa. . . .' (I looked it up later: capital of the Bashkir Republic, 400 miles east of Moscow, on the route of the Trans-Siberian Railway. Rudolf never went into details.) 'My mother only could get two tickets, so I had to stay at home.' (His sister got the other.) 'Somehow I succeeded to go. There was big crowd outside and I went in between legs. When I saw dance, I said, *"That is what I want to do."* '

I said something about determination.

'Gave chess up at age twelve,' he said. 'Too slow! And chequers, cards, any game. If it didn't happen quick, I'd slam board. Got violent. Too slow!' He gave me a bit of a stare. 'I bet you play chess.'

'Yes.'

'Yes. I bet you play very slowly too.' Then his mind made a typically sudden knight's move. 'I never gambled. Sometimes when I dance near casino, public would put my name on chips, and I hope they lose.' Something-for-nothing offended him. In his world, if you didn't sweat for it, you didn't deserve it.

He had quite a large scar on his left upper lip. How did that happen?

'When I was child I shared bread ration with dog. Dog jumped up and seized my lip with jaws.' He smiled in a way that showed off the scar. 'Not nice way for dog to treat me.'

He skimmed rapidly through his years at the Kirov Ballet School. It was as if he was on autopilot: he'd told his story so often that the anecdotes were compressed into brief

135

bunches of words. Then he got to his 1961 defection, when the Kirov Ballet was at the end of its Paris tour, and the company had gathered at Le Bourget airport, and he made what Fleet Street felt compelled to call his 'leap for freedom'. The myth endures; on 14 January 1997, BBC television broadcast an *Omnibus* programme on Nureyev, during which Patricia Ruanne, ballet mistress for Rudolf when he was artistic director at the Paris Opéra in the 1980s, commented on his reasons for taking the job: 'Paris seemed a logical place – he had jumped over the barrier here.' Elizabeth Kay, a writer, went further:

> The day he defected, I remember it coming on the radio, and it was 'the leap to freedom' – and it was *so* romantic; and it was this combination of the political leap and the dancer's leap! And what it did for Rudolf was it made him an international celebrity before he'd ever danced more than one night in the West.

Alas, the facts don't fit the legend: Nureyev had danced throughout the Kirov Paris tour before he defected; and he insisted that there was no 'dancer's leap' at the airport.

'Rubbish. Absolute rubbish! Didn't leap over barrier. No dancer jumps in suit! One would hurt oneself! No jumping, no shouting, no running. How can you run? You're dancer, you don't run.' The company was due to fly on to London. Nureyev's Paris debut had been highly successful. The Kirov management thought he was too big for his boots and too free with his opinions, so the tour's KGB minders produced a different plan for him. 'They said, no room for me on that plane. Said, you go back and dance for Khrushchev at Kremlin. I knew that was lie.' Nureyev was convinced he would be exiled to some remote corner of the USSR. 'I went to French police and said, "I want to stay in your country." They said, "Take six steps in this direction.' I did. That was all."

In fact, witnesses said there was a certain amount of shouting and cursing, especially when a Russian woman interpreter threatened that his family would suffer, and he snapped, 'You shut up, you bitch!' – which probably sounds better in Russian. But Nureyev insisted that his defection was no big drama. What stuck in his mind and still upset him, thirty years on, was that the tour managers sent his baggage back to Leningrad and dumped it in his room at the Kirov. Years later, Baryshnikov was given the same room and (Nureyev said) took the bags. 'Baryshnikov had my clothes,' he used to complain. He wasn't joking. He felt the loss. When he defected, his clothes were all he owned.

Nureyev could have had any food he liked. What he ate was risotto. Endlessly.

Soon after we arrived, the builder – Benito Fusco – turned up with his wife. She offered to make risotto for lunch. Rudolf said, 'Good! Show Blue how.' But when she began cooking he stopped her. 'No. You stand beside. Make him learn.'

Signora Fusco had a fit of the giggles. 'You must stir often,' she told me.

Rudolf said, 'If you must stir often, don't stop stirring.' Then he left us to it.

Signora Fusco taught me how to make Milanese risotto. Since Nureyev virtually lived on it, and since he believed that good dance was impossible without good food, the recipe might be worth noting.

Get a good thick-bottomed pan, melt a knob of butter an inch square and add as much olive oil. Chop a white onion. Fry it gently until it softens. It must not go brown. Pour in a cup of risotto rice. Cook it on a low heat, stirring it often, so that it soaks up the oil and butter, until the grains start to heat up. (Don't use long-grain rice. Use Italian Arborio Risotto rice, which has short, squat grains. If you can't get it, English pudding rice is the next best thing.) Now you need a litre of hot chicken stock, or you can make it with a stock cube. Add a bit – half a cup, say – and stir with a wooden spoon. Keep stirring. It should have made a lot of steam. After a few minutes, when the stock's absorbed, add a bit more. Stir. Keep stirring. Never cover the pan. Always stir. You might need a bit more stock, or add some white wine. The trick with risotto is to add the liquid gradually and never neglect it. Rush it by pouring in too much stock, and you get something like bad tapioca. Stop stirring and let it stick and it tastes like burnt toast. Good risotto can easily take thirty or forty minutes to make. It has a wonderful tangy taste, a slightly crunchy texture, and the washing-up is easy because nothing has stuck to the pan. Risotto doesn't need garlic. Rudolf liked a little pepper, a lot of salt, and grated parmesan sprinkled on top. He reckoned he needed a scrape whenever he ate risotto because it's such a rich dish. In one period I cooked risotto for him thirty days in a row.

And all the time, Nureyev might explode at any minute, shattering into fragments of theatrical temperament which had to be carefully rebuilt.

Sometimes he had a small war with a faraway enemy, in which case he never lost his self-control and he usually won (although it was hard to see what good these little victories did him). He especially enjoyed making sudden raids on distant ballet companies. He attacked by fax. We were on Li Galli when he dictated a fax to the director of La Scala, Milan, abruptly withdrawing all production of his ballets as long as Carboni worked there. Rudolf knew that La Scala was just about to present one of his ballets. He also remembered Carboni from Verona, where he had directed *Death in Venice*. There was a flurry of faxes and phone calls from Milan, and the ballet went ahead.

He also tossed a hand grenade into the Royal Ballet.

In those days it was headed by Jeremy Isaacs. Rudolf asked, 'Is Jeremy Isaacs a sir or a lord?' I thought he was plain mister. Rudolf dictated a fax to all three: *Dear Mr, Sir or Lord Isaacs.* . . . He accused the Royal Ballet of not having paid him fees amounting to $10,000, leaving him so poor that 'I now do not think I will be able to hire a taxi to Covent Garden,' so he immediately withdrew from the Royal Ballet his production of the ballet *Raymonda* which (he claimed) they'd had 'for twenty-seven years without paying me any rewards.'

He had a similarly dark suspicion that he was being cheated out of repeat fees by *The Muppet Show*. A dozen years before, he had guested on the show, dancing with Miss Piggy (who wore a tutu) in *Swine Lake*. That show was much repeated. 'Must check on my royalties,' Rudolf said whenever the Muppets were mentioned. 'Don't think I'm getting them.'

Of course he had agents to take care of all that stuff, but he distrusted his agents – or he liked to pretend that he did. Luigi Pignotti was usually the victim. Rudolf never spared him, even when – especially when – Rudolf had demanded the impossible and Luigi could not deliver. 'Traitor!' Rudolf snarled, and hung up the phone. For the next few days, Rudolf would be calling people, saying, 'Big divorce with Luigi. Never again will I speak to him.' It happened a lot.

Yet when a genuine mini-crisis blew up, he was completely unruffled.

Li Galli

It was later in the summer, when occasional visitors came to stay. One was a delightful Frenchwoman, Marie Suzanne. She was a secretary at the Paris Opéra (where he had been director). Many people misunderstood Nureyev's attitude towards women: they assumed that such a thoroughgoing homosexual could not share his life with a woman, especially a good-looking woman. That was not true. Marie Suzanne was a few years older, elegant, intelligent, attractive, and she brought all the latest gossip from the dance world, which he welcomed; but most of all she had a rare quality of *lightness*. Too many heavy people weighed down Rudolf's life. Marie Suzanne was light. She was fun. She and Rudolf were the best of friends.

One of the heavyweights was an Italian whom I'll call Pietro, because that was not his name. He was a top stage designer. He arrived with his secretary. Rudolf said they would stay for three or four days. I said I hoped they liked risotto. Pietro ate risotto but he also ate everything else. That's what caused the mini-crisis. He was not light. He was a stiff, unsmiling man and he ignored everyone but Rudolf. You had to be very self-centred to ignore people on such a tiny island, but Pietro did it. He worked with Rudolf, discussing stage designs, and several times a day he went to the kitchen and raided the fridge. At this rate we would soon run out of food.

Marie Suzanne had an idea. 'Put something in front of the fridge,' she suggested. 'See what he thinks.' I placed two brooms across the fridge door, and Pietro erupted in flames.

'Never in all my life have I been so insulted!' he told me. 'I leave *now*. Get me a boat now.' And he stormed off.

I went to Rudolf, explained everything, apologized for offending his guest. Rudolf didn't even blink. 'If he wants dramatics, he can go,' he said.

I found Pietro, and apologized. 'An English joke,' I said. He gave me a hard stare. Maybe he suspected that the apology was another English joke.

'Never have I been so insulted,' he said. A great designer, but short on dialogue. Marie Suzanne confirmed to him that it was an English joke.

'It's not funny,' he told her; but he decided not to go.

Rudolf was poker-faced. 'Oh well ... Have we enough food? OK. Carry on.' He might even have been slightly disappointed. In thirty years of ballet he'd seen much bigger fits of temperament.

But whereas the loss of a brilliant stage designer didn't bother him, being deprived of a pair of pink shorts did, very much. And they weren't even his shorts.

Clothes were no problem for Nureyev: he had them stashed away in every house he owned. By contrast, I had to carry everything I wore. He got bored with my basic wardrobe – green corduroys and a shirt. 'Your clothes are very uninteresting,' he said. First chance I had, I bought some bright striped trousers. Rudolf approved. That was fine. Then he tried to borrow a pair of shorts. I resisted. That was not fine. That was stormy.

Guests were coming for lunch, and Rudolf wanted to look good. He said, 'Blue, do you have any shorts I can wear?' We both knew he had plenty of shorts. He wanted mine. 'What about those pink shorts?' he said. I'd just washed this baggy pink pair. I tried to steer him away.

'Can't I look out a pair of yours?' I said.

Big mistake. Bad move. Storm clouds arrived. He said, 'So you don't want me to wear. . . .' Thunder rumbled, lightning flashed. He snarled, 'You be mean to me, *I'll* be mean to you.' It was like a playground squabble, except that to Rudolf it was life and death. I said I'd get the shorts.

'No, no, no, no, no.' We were through. I was a traitor. We were divorced.

I talked him round, and he agreed, grudgingly, to wear the damn shorts. If I hadn't given in, that would have been the end: I would have been sacked.

I should have known better than to resist. The world revolved around Rudolf, and to try to deny this was to risk tipping the world off its axis. It was trivial, childish; it was only a pair of pink shorts; but not to get them meant that his world was briefly reversed; and that, for him, was intolerable.

But if tiny deprivations infuriated Nureyev, tiny gifts delighted him hugely.

He clumped around Li Galli in heavy yellow clogs, until he went swimming and lost one. We were going to Capri for the day, and I said I'd like to buy him some clogs. 'Oh!' he said. He never got sunburned but the sun made his cheeks apple-red; now they glowed with anticipated pleasure. 'Thank you very much.' But when we got to Capri there were no clogs to be found. 'How about buying me a sweatshirt?' he said.

I bought him a cheery sweatshirt. He was as bucked as a boy on a new bicycle. Things like that revealed the other side of Nureyev. They compensated for outbursts like the storm over the pink shorts. They made you feel protective, because the man so obviously needed protection, despite the fact that he was by instinct aggressive.

On Li Galli, he watched a lot of videos, especially Fred Astaire movies. ('Look at his feet. Great talent! A master.') He liked the Marx Brothers best. They made him howl with laughter. The gross puns, the sparring word play, the insults, the put-downs: he couldn't get enough of them. But Nureyev's own humour could be even blacker. One night we were watching a television documentary about wildlife in the Florida swamps. Somebody tossed a dead sheep into the water. At once there was a frenzy of alligators feeding on it. 'Ah!' Rudolf said. 'Paris Opéra.'

One evening, at dinner, I asked if he knew dancers with truly great ability who nevertheless never succeeded. He nodded. 'They lack something here.' He pointed to his forehead. 'Will, determination ... But I have decided to be conductor, so I *will* be conductor. I told Luigi – don't interfere with my conducting. I would kill my mother if she interrupted.'

We rarely went to the mainland, but he made one trip to dance in an open-air production of *L'après-midi d'un faune*. It was being presented by an Italian lady whose son had recently died in a dreadful car crash. This was the first time Rudolf had met her since the tragedy. He said, 'I'm very sorry to hear about him, but – work conquers all.' He wasn't trivializing her grief. He believed what he said. The answer to death was life, and life meant effort. He worked furiously hard to become a conductor. If he was unwell or weary, he seemed to work twice as hard. There was no obstacle that could not be overcome by effort, by willpower.

13

Vienna
More Than a Famous Name

Death was not a career move that Nureyev was willing to consider.

He couldn't dance – certainly not in the way that his name evoked – and choreography and directing were second-best options. Also they didn't give him top billing. Nureyev had always been in the limelight, and that's where he wanted to stay. He wanted to conduct, and he'd been manoeuvring discreetly in that direction for some time. The crunch came in May 1991, during the British tour, when he came face to face with Dr Franz Moser. Rudolf called him 'the smiling poodle' because he had tightly curled hair, but he said it only to me. Rudolf needed Moser; needed him badly. Moser was his best hope for a second career.

Rudolf was staying at Maude Gosling's house in Kensington when Moser arrived from Vienna: a tall, slim man in his thirties who did, in fact, smile a lot. With him was a young Austrian conductor. They went into another room and, very courteously, they grilled Rudolf for five hours – all afternoon until the early evening.

This in itself was extraordinary: Rudolf rarely gave inter-views, and when he did they were brief. Furthermore his tour schedule was very tight. But what Moser wanted, Moser got. He was the director of Palais Auersperg in Vienna. This is a handsome palace with rooms so large that they can be used as concert halls. The place houses a musi-cal organization that plays a lot of Mozart, employs a lot of musicians and has a lot of cultural clout. That clout would be improved by adding the name of Nureyev. In return, the Palais Auersperg could give Rudolf his start as a conductor – provided that Moser and his colleague believed that Rudolf was a good bet.

He convinced them. They came out of the meeting with a verbal agreement. Now Rudolf had what every appren-tice conductor dreams of: an orchestra to practise on, free. Good; bully for him. Presumably the others believed what Rudolf believed: that a great career on the rostrum stretched before him. A little over a year and a half after that meeting, he was dead.

Probably Dr Moser had never seen Nureyev in the flesh before they met in London and therefore he had no chance to observe the physical changes so obvious to people like Luigi. Yet Moser was no fool. Even if Nureyev was less than frank about his medical condition – and to my knowledge he discussed it with nobody except Dr Canesi – there was plenty of gossip. The gossip was inspired by Nureyev's notorious lifestyle and by his appearance. For instance, he had always been concerned about draughts, and as the year wore on, that concern became more of a dread. If we were in a restaurant he might sneeze and draw his shawl more tightly around himself, and people at nearby tables would glance significantly at each other in a way that said AIDS. It's hard to believe that the gossip hadn't reached Vienna. Once, at a dinner party on Capri, when I discreetly gave him his AZT pill, he waved it around so that all the guests could see. He was flaunting his condition, parading it as something trivial. His stamina was legendary; perhaps he really believed that he was indestructible. Perhaps Moser believed so too.

In midsummer we left Li Galli for Vienna. Rudolf was to fly from Naples; I would go by train. For some reason he decided to buy my ticket himself, so we both went to the railway station. It would have been much easier to give me the money and tell me to make my own way, but he was not in a trusting mood. He probably had a walletful of lire, which always made him suspicious. He was also going to the airport, which made him jumpy. It all added up to the wrong frame of mind in which to set about buying an Italian railway ticket.

Rudolf got the first bit right: he walked straight to the head of the queue. This was quite natural for him; he always did it. Russian ballet stars regard it as their right. When Irek Mukhamedov left the Bolshoi for the Royal Ballet, during his first lunch break he went to the head of the queue in the canteen. He had never stood in line in Russia, and he was utterly taken aback by the uproar. Mukhamedov retreated to his proper place. Rudolf never did. He always got away with it. People frowned and muttered, but he seemed to radiate some unarguable right to be first.

He said, 'I want an overnight sleeper to Vienna, from here.'

Nothing is that simple in Italy. The ticket clerk said, 'Well, you can go by Rome . . . or you can go by Milan . . . or on the other hand you can—'

'*Nev mind dat. Vienna!*'

'Well. . . . How do you want to go, sir?'

Rudolf snapped, '*Vienna*!'

'Yes, sir. The point is—'

'*Vienna Vienna Vienna*!' Fury had gripped Rudolf's brain. He seemed about to throw a punch. Instead he grabbed his money. 'You – fly with me!' We ran to the car.

The more furious and frustrated he got, the more he demanded speed. He was off to Vienna to start a new career. He could do this because he was convinced he was going to live a very long life. So every second counted. That's how his mind worked.

Rudolf had a serious flaw of character. In the world of the arts he had to be perfect. He couldn't admit a mistake.

In other areas of life he didn't care what people thought of his inadequacies. He couldn't tie a necktie, he couldn't change a lightbulb, he couldn't write a letter, he couldn't grill a steak. None of these things mattered. Dance mattered, and there Rudolf was in his element, fearless, utterly self-assured.

Now, in Vienna, with a baton in his hand, he was out of his element and he was very twitchy. This was like going back to school and Rudolf was as nervous as a new boy. He was very suspicious of the musicians. They were professionals who knew he was a beginner. They would notice every mistake he made. Even worse, they would spot mistakes he didn't *know* he'd made. The world of orchestras is full of stories of conductors made to look foolish by musicians, especially at rehearsals.

Rudolf was highly sensitive to any hint of ridicule. He knew they knew far more than he did. Suppose he told them to do the wrong thing? What then? And it was inevitable that he would do just that, because learning meant making mistakes, perhaps looking foolish, and Rudolf had absolutely no talent for looking foolish in

148

public. So he was very, very cautious. If a musician had so much as rolled his eyes, Rudolf would have been on the next plane to Naples.

He was saved by Wilhelm Hubener, whom everyone called Papa.

He was a Viennese violinist, sixty-something, energetic and warm-hearted and a great believer in Rudolf's talents. The first conducting sessions were held at his house in the country, using only three or four musicians, all carefully selected by Papa. They took Rudolf seriously, and as soon as he recognized their respect for him, his nervousness faded and his confidence grew. So did the size of the group, and they moved to a rehearsal room in the palace.

One day he was conducting and he made a complete hash of it. He went one way and the orchestra went another. Big blunder. Everyone stopped, and his face turned bright red. It was just like the day when the lady from *The New York Times* found him stark naked, except that now he couldn't back out of the room. But although some people smiled, nobody laughed; and Rudolf got his act together, and they began again. Progress.

Papa's son was in California, so we stayed at his flat when we weren't living in an apartment off Palais Auersperg. Papa's wife Lydia was Russian-born, an ex-opera singer, now pushing sixty. Life had not been easy for them – in one of Rudolf's favourite phrases, they had 'learned to over-come' – and he felt very relaxed in their company. Lydia cooked us wonderful Russian meals. She cooked so many of them that Rudolf tried to take the Hubeners out to dinner.

'No, no,' she said. 'There's no point in spending a thou-sand schillings and then flushing it down the sewer next morning.'

Rudolf laughed, and gave in.

He was sleeping more and more. In Vienna he spent at least twelve hours a day in bed. When he was awake, his success at Palais Auersperg gave him a new vitality. I drove him from the apartment to the palace by the most direct route. It bored him. 'Why d'you keep taking me this shit way? Take me where there's flowers. Something to see.' He also told me to go to a new production of *The Magic Flute*. I said I was tired. 'Forget tired! You'll never see this again.' He was very perky.

But then, he had every right to be perky. Considering that he had never before conducted anybody, anywhere, Nureyev now had everything he needed. He had musicians to practise with, other conductors to learn from, rehearsal space of high quality, and all in a richly musical setting. He had the enthusiastic backing of Franz Moser and the sympathetic advice of Papa Hubener. His agreement with the Palais Auersperg was open-ended: if it worked, there was no limit to his success. They even got their tailor to make him white tie and tails, in readiness for his first performance. Rudolf said, 'Who pays?' Moser said the palace would pay. Rudolf didn't smile, but he twitched his eyebrows. Life was good.

When Rudolf wasn't sleeping, he was working. He never wasted a minute. I videotaped his conducting sessions, and when we got home he studied his performance, usually with Papa Hubener alongside. And, of course, Rudolf contrived to have a scrape every day, if possible. In the mornings he could barely get out of bed but nothing slowed him down. He'd got what he wanted and now he was making the most of it.

It was exciting to be surrounded by so many brilliant musicians, and I took my chances too. A lady violinist at Palais Auersperg gave me a free lesson on the violin. After half an hour my left arm got cramps, which amused her. And I got to know Howard Penny, a wonderful cellist; he too gave me a lesson. It was no fun for anyone within earshot. I gave up.

Vienna was hard work but enjoyable. Rudolf didn't complain much, so presumably he was satisfied. It was easy to tell when he was pleased, because he suddenly flowered. It had happened on Capri with the cheery sweatshirt. Now it happened in Vienna with six pairs of black socks.

He had been thirty years in the West, and people sent him gifts from all over: roses, or huge boxes of Belgian chocolates, or cases of champagne. Rudolf was an isolated and lonely person, but this high-priced stuff just made him feel even more remote. What Rudolf Nureyev wanted was a gift that *meant* something.

When he had a scrape, he pulled socks over his dance shoes. This extended their life, but all his socks had holes. Now Papa Hubener and Dr Moser were talking about his first concert, and he had no black socks. I bought him six pairs.

This small gift moved him, to a degree that can only be called joy. It was touchingly easy to make Rudolf happy: you just had to be a little bit kind to him. No fanfares; he'd had fanfares. But how long was it since anyone gave him socks?

The day came when he wore the black socks, and the white tie and tails, and conducted a full-scale concert at Palais Auersperg. It was a complete success. Everyone was enormously pleased; Nureyev wasn't just a famous name on a podium, he was clearly a man with an understanding of music and the talent to help others create it. Papa's efforts had been rewarded and Dr Moser's faith was justified. Rudolf, of course, was hugely relieved, and as soon as the congratulations were over he was eager to consolidate his success.

He and Papa sat around the Hubeners' kitchen table and made plans, while Lydia prepared steak tartare or cooked white sausage – two of Rudolf's favourites. The plans soon came good. Nureyev was in demand. He conducted more and bigger concerts in Vienna, and again he was well received. He conducted orchestras on a short tour to Hungary, and made a similar tour of Greece. I didn't go with him on those trips, but I know he came back feeling very satisfied. His reputation was spreading. It even reached Bulgaria, and a crew from Bulgarian television arrived to film him. Elsewhere in Europe, and in the United States, there was interest in engaging the services of Nureyev the conductor. His bandwagon was rolling again.

All this effort, however, had cost him a lot in strength and stamina. He couldn't maintain the pace indefinitely. Before the next burst of activity he needed a break from Palais Auersperg, and the obvious place to go was Li Galli.

He was tired, but he was far from exhausted. We hadn't got onto the island before sex reared its pretty little head again. Rudolf never knew when to quit.

14

Stormy Weather

Food, the KGB and Bedtime Rituals

Climbing from any boat on to a dock can be awkward. The boat may be rising and falling, the concrete is wet or greasy or both. When we landed on Li Galli my routine was to throw the bags ashore, plant one foot on the dock while I kept the other in the boat and then lift Rudolf onto the island.

First, however, I had to grab a chain fixed to the dock. As I did so, Rudolf pinched my ass. We got ashore and I said, 'Rudolf, I thought you promised that that sort of thing was no-go?'

He gave his wide-eyed Tartar look and a bit of a smile and shrugged. It had been a freebie. He couldn't resist it.

Well, it was only a pinch. Did it matter so much? Yes, it mattered. Nureyev's nature was to be as self-indulgent as he could get away with. I could be physically close to him seven days a week only if we were emotionally distant from each other. The trouble was, like Oscar Wilde, Nureyev could resist anything except temptation. And if he thought he could get away with a pinch on the ass, he would assume that I was his for the taking. That's what made it hard to live with Nureyev. He made the rules, and then he tried to unmake them whenever it suited him. He couldn't be trusted.

It was an odd life.

After the intense activity in Vienna, Rudolf switched back to his isolated, introverted routine. His daily pattern was a scrape, a plunge, and hours and hours of playing Bach on the piano or studying tapes and scores of classical music. He was a recluse. Yet at any moment he was liable to ask a question that demanded an instant answer. And of course it was not possible to disagree with him. To argue was to challenge, and since Rudolf was never wrong, a challenge was tantamount to treason. The most I could ever say was, 'My experience has been different. . . .' Rudolf's mind was made up. He didn't want it unmade.

In some ways Li Galli was wonderful. Eating dinner on the balcony while the sun went down over the Mediterranean was a glorious experience . . . provided you could forget the fact that Rudolf had been wearing the same clothes for a week, or perhaps two weeks, or more, and they badly needed to be washed. When he found clothes that he liked (often mine), he just wore them endlessly; he couldn't be persuaded to put on something else while they were laundered. Either he liked his clothes to be dirty or he didn't care; probably the latter. On the other hand, there was always the possibility of excitement: we might get invited to lunch with Gore Vidal at Ravello, just up the coast, or a high-speed launch might arrive to take us to a dinner party on Capri. As often as not, Rudolf turned down these invitations; he preferred solitude and my risotto. And when it came to housekeeping money, he was still as tight-fisted as ever. Greed is one of the less attractive peasant qualities. In his case it had a stupid, self-destructive streak, because the main person he was shortchanging was himself. There were times when I couldn't pay the grocer in Positano. Yet Nureyev could have *bought* the grocer. He could have bought the street.

Benito Fusco, the contractor in charge of the tiling work, recognized the situation. From time to time he gave me cash. He'd pat me on the shoulder and say, 'This is for your float, Blue.' At first it was bewildering, this topsy-turvy arrangement, and I protested.

Benito said, 'That's OK. I know you haven't enough to go shopping. This is how I work.'

I was grateful: now I needn't worry about buying luxuries like rice and toilet paper. I massaged my conscience with the assumption that these handouts were somehow absorbed in the building costs. I got that wrong: utterly wrong. Benito Fusco and his men worked hard for Nureyev, and in return Nureyev treated Benito very shabbily. But that came later, when we were off the island.

It was pointless to ask Rudolf for more money; he would have said what he always said 'You will overcome.' Which meant: no.

At Palais Auersperg, he had worked with a sizeable orchestra. One day they turned up at Li Galli, all forty of them. They were on tour in Italy, so they hired a boat and visited us.

'Lunch in one hour,' Rudolf told me. 'For fifty.'

In fact it was only forty-five, including some guests already there. Lettuce grew on our terraces, so a couple of musicians picked lettuce. I made risotto for forty-five. Forty minutes later we ate lunch. Rudolf said nothing to me when the orchestra left. From his point of view, nothing special had happened.

Howard Penny – the brilliant Australian cellist who gave me a free lesson in Vienna – stayed on Li Galli for a few days. He thought long and hard before accepting the invitation; after all, he would be trapped on a very small island with this notorious seducer of men. I assured him that Rudolf was interested only in his music and his wit; still, Howard made sure that I too would be on Li Galli before he said yes. He enjoyed his stay, but he was bewildered by the episode of the salmon steaks.

They were for lunch. Rudolf reckoned I always overcooked them. This time he gave orders: *'Undercook* salmon. Bring it to me. I'll tell you.'

He and Howard were having a glass of wine when I brought the salmon on two plates. Naturally Howard thought lunch was about to be served. Rudolf looked at the fish and said, 'No.' It was a long journey to the kitchen – across the patio and down a flight of a dozen stairs. However, I put the salmon back in the oven, took it out, made the return journey, showed him. Same result. This happened six times. By now Howard was utterly baffled. At the sixth inspection Rudolf said, 'Almost.'

I gave it another minute, and when I served it that salmon was as near perfect as a salmon will ever be. Unfortunately Howard was so shaken by the whole experience that he found it hard to eat. Four years later we bumped into each other in Australia, and he was still amazed that Rudolf had – as he thought – treated me so badly.

I tried to explain that there had been nothing humiliating about it. We had simply concentrated on achieving a good performance. Now I'm not so sure. My job was to bring some stability to Rudolf's life: I was the male nurse in the mental hospital. Maybe I had spent so long in his abnormal company that I was beginning to be affected by it. Maybe it was time to back out while I could still find the exit.

Howard left. Life resumed its lonely routine, with one big difference. Rudolf Nureyev taught me to dance. Not many people can say that. Unfortunately not even Rudolf Nureyev could teach me to dance *well*; but he gave me eight lessons on Li Galli; and that was remarkably generous of him.

After the free violin and cello lessons in Vienna, I asked him if there was any chance of a dance lesson. He made his usual instant decision. 'Yes. Don't talk to me. I'll do my steps. You stand behind me. Do as I do. Or the nearest you can.' We went to the Tower.

Forty minutes of scrape left me drenched in sweat. I felt like a wounded buffalo. He looked like a thoughtful gazelle. At the end, when I was wobbling, he said, 'This must be like Chinese to you, the way feet move so fast.' And he told me what I must achieve: 'Contact with floor. Push your foot almost through floor. That's how you educate feet.'

Occasionally Rudolf talked about ballet. 'My advice for young dancers is to give up,' he said. 'If they can, they are not missed.'

And if they can't?

'Then there is something. It's much too easy for dancers today.'

Really? It doesn't *look* easy.

'Some have perfect steps. Technically they are good. That's not enough. You must bring something. Passion. Get passion from music, put it in dance.' When Rudolf joined the Royal Ballet in the early sixties, it became obvious that some other dancers were not bringing enough passion to their performances. 'Press called me "Cuckooshka",' he said, 'because I threw all out of nest.' His stamina then was apparently inexhaustible: in the sixties he gave two hundred and fifty performances a year, plus choreography, directing and television work. He was a dynamo. 'People not know how to spell name,' he said, 'so I called myself Randolph Neveroff.'

Nureyev's dancing was dazzlingly athletic, especially the leaps. Even on film, they look impossible. It seems as if he could poise in mid-air. 'You train yourself,' he said. 'You jump and you extend.' He gestured: one leg stretched forward, the other back. 'Keep legs horizontal and arms still. And you freeze. Freeze before top point of jump. Now body is motionless. Don't move any part of body. So.'

Rugby players leap for the ball at line-outs. The best line-out jumpers seem to hang in the air at the top of their leap. They have the advantage of going up vertically, whereas dancers leap *across* the stage. 'You should have played rugby,' I told him. 'You'd have made a great line-out jumper.'

'Eediott.'

In the second lesson I attempted an *entrechat*. Dancers do it all the time: they jump, the legs criss-cross at the lower calf, they land. It was utterly impossible. Rudolf said there was no trick to it. 'Just footwork. Not height of jump. Got to get feet moving.' On the way out of the Tower he said, 'Nijinsky did *entrechat dix*, with his little legs.'

Ten? *Ten* of them?

'I did *entrechat dix* but just toes overlapping. Nijinsky did whole foot overlapping. Phenomenal.'

In the third lesson I nearly achieved one *entrechat*. 'Good!' Rudolf shouted. In the fifth lesson I got very close. 'Ah!' he said. 'Your mother would be very surprised.' It was a typically enigmatic remark. During the sixth lesson, Gore

Vidal strolled in. He enjoyed watching Rudolf at work, but I felt a little foolish. 'I'm afraid I haven't any talent, Mr Vidal,' I said.

'Don't worry,' he said. 'Many careers have been made like that.'

Occasionally a boat anchored off the island. I always got the binoculars out, just in case it might be another orchestra arriving for lunch. Late one afternoon I focused on a yacht that had dropped anchor. Heather and Neil were on board. The same Heather and Neil with whom I'd crossed the Pacific on *Keama*.

Rudolf was willing to meet them, so they came ashore. I was surprised at the great excitement I felt. What surprised *them* was how tired I looked. (That wasn't news: Luigi and Howard and others had said the same.) Heather and Neil were delivering the yacht to Naples. They brought news of friends, especially of Jane who was keen to know when we would meet again.

Rudolf chatted with them. Then, when he was elsewhere for a moment, Neil invited me to spend a night on the boat, sail to Capri, have a beer or two, come back first thing next morning. 'The boss won't even notice you've gone,' he said.

That seemed very unlikely. Still, I went and found him and told him of the invitation. Big, big mistake.

Rudolf straightened up. '*How long*? How long will you go?'

Overnight, I said. Just overnight. Back early tomorrow.

'*When*? When you leave?' I said I'd go whenever they were ready.

'Oh!' His fuse began to burn. It was a very short fuse. 'What am I going to do for dinner? You're going to abandon me? How do I cook?' He began screaming. '*Well! That's great! Abandon me! Go off, as soon as the drop of a hat! Fine! You*

159

go off with your friends! What am I supposed to do about food? On my own? Here?' And he stormed off.

Heather and Neil had heard all this. They were shocked by the outburst, and I could tell Heather was upset by his anger. They went back to the boat. I went back to Rudolf. He was still in a rage.

'How can you *ask* things like that? You *know* you work for me! You *know* I need. . . .' His anger outran his words.

He had to be soothed like a child. He had to be calmed and reassured. The technique was simple: it involved saying simple things, softly and gently, over and over again, until the distress went away. 'Of course I won't go, Rudolf. Of course I won't go. Rudolf, if you don't want me to go, I won't go. I won't go. I'll stay here. I wasn't telling you I was going, Rudolf. I just asked. I only asked you, Rudolf. Only a question. I'm staying here, Rudolf. Of course I won't go. . . .'

After a while his face lost its anguished look and he grunted a bit. 'Hmmm. Mmmm. Mmmm. OK.'

'I'm not going. Just a question.'

'OK.' He picked up a book. The crisis was over.

I walked to the tail of the island and watched the yacht motor away. Heather was obviously upset, which meant bad news for Jane. Nothing could be done about that. I went back and cooked an especially good dinner. What's more, I was especially cheerful during the meal. Surprisingly, so was Rudolf.

But it had been touch-and-go for both of us. He might have fired me; I might have quit. With every month that passed, there were more reasons for going and fewer reasons for staying. One reason for going was the evidence that Rudolf was no longer the person who had hired me. As his body wasted away, so his mind began losing its strength. Even then, on Li Galli, I could see that the time would come when I would be no help to him and he would be no help to me.

It was a purely professional relationship. If I had broken my leg he would have fired me on the spot. I felt far more protective towards him than he did towards me; for instance, I defended him vigorously whenever he was mocked or criticized behind his back. But when the job I was doing ceased to be the job I had agreed to do, I would go.

The man was a genius. He had earned the right to live an extraordinary life

Nevertheless . . . why was he so fragile? Why did an apparently trivial suggestion – the idea, on St Barts, of my taking a quick shower before cooking dinner – bring on such an explosion of fury? He seemed to be motoring smoothly through life. Why should he strip his gears over nothing very much? Part of the answer must be that, to Nureyev, it wasn't nothing very much. So what was it? Here are some tentative conclusions.

Nureyev communicated by dance. What he ate influenced how he danced. There is a well-told story of Rudolf and Margot on an American tour, guests at a lunch where the main dish was chicken, and not very good chicken at that. According to him, she said, 'Chicken lunch, chicken performance.' (According to her, he said it.) What's more, Rudolf's body sometimes burned up energy with astonishing speed. Maude Gosling told me that when Rudolf stayed at her house, during his first year in London, he could be sitting, doing nothing, and suddenly burst into sweat for no apparent reason. There were times when Maude and her husband, Nigel, would leave the house to take him to Covent Garden when a sudden ravenous hunger would overcome Rudolf, even though he had recently eaten. They had to turn back, and Maude cooked something fast, like scrambled eggs. Then Rudolf was OK again, and went and danced up a storm.

So food was enormously important to him. He'd grown up in Russia when nobody could be certain of tomorrow's meal, and the preoccupation never left him. Working with damaged children taught me that food can be a more powerful means of communication than speech. Sometimes it's the only means of communication.

Two of Rudolf's big explosions – on St Barts (*You work for me, I don't work for you!*) and on Li Galli (*You're going to abandon me? How do I cook?*) – concerned food. His needs for food were simple, but the slightest threat to them was like a threat to his life. This revealed a massive insecurity. He was a good actor, he had a good poker-face; but under strain he broke out in rage, or panic. It was the story of his life: Nureyev against the world. A glimpse of this emerged when he talked about the KGB.

He defected at the height of the Cold War, when there was deep distrust between East and West; and for a while people in the West suspected that *he* was a KGB agent. (Certainly that thought passed through Margot Fonteyn's mind.) Success did not remove the suspicion. Quite soon, he bought a house in Monte Carlo and paid cash. He'd earned it by dancing – but many people thought it must be KGB money. All the while, Rudolf was afraid that the KGB would kidnap him, maybe even murder him.

That fear never completely left him. When in London he always stayed in the basement flat at Maude's house. It had an old-style dial phone. When you picked it up, it clicked. 'See?' Rudolf said. 'KGB.' It was no joke. Rudolf never joked about the KGB. 'See?' he said. 'They're still listening.' He was convinced of it. After thirty years in the West, Rudolf was afraid. You have to be Russian to understand such insecurity. It was bred in the bone. Something else contributed to Rudolf's fragility. It was his incurable distrust. He was a perfectionist: so he distrusted everyone. Given half a chance, people would let him down. They always did. Look here: his cook was threatening to vanish to Capri and leave him to starve! Might never come back!

Rudolf trusted nobody except himself. That was his great strength. It could also be a terrible and exhausting weakness.

Life with Nureyev was always life on a knife-edge. You had to live it in order to know how sharp the edge was. Tiny details assumed large significance.

There was a routine to the end of the working day. Rudolf said, 'I'm going to sleep now.' He shuffled off and sat on the edge of the bed while I went around, turning off lights. Then I said, 'Goodnight, Rudolf.'

'Goodnight.' A pause, and softly, 'Oh . . . thank you.' That was an indicator of harmony, a signal that he was content. Then, for no apparent reason, it stopped.

We were on St Barts. I said my 'Goodnight, Rudolf', and he said nothing. Not even a grunt. And being Rudolf, he didn't say what he was annoyed or upset or worried about. About a month later – a month in which nothing obvious had changed – I said goodnight and he spoke again: 'Oh . . . thank you.' A certain tension vanished, and I never knew why.

Another indicator was his after-dinner remark. When I cleared the table I always said, 'Can I get you anything?' He might ask for an apple; but three or four nights a week he said, 'Big dick.'

'Salted or unsalted?'

'Unsalted.'

It was a comic routine, part of the coarse Tartar image he

liked to project. It was an encouraging sign: it meant that he felt relaxed and at ease. Rudolf's profanity was always an encouraging sign. Luigi was a big man, and Rudolf enjoyed making fun of his *zhoppa* – Italian slang for backside: 'Luigi! Move that big fat *zhoppa* of yours!' Rudolf liked swearing. He did it to brighten up a dull conversation and for the fun of shocking people. He never said, 'Sit down.' He said, 'Shit you down.' If it embarrassed the other person, good; that amused Rudolf. *Shit you down* embarrassed Margot, and according to Rudolf she was pretty unshockable. So he kept on saying it.

Shit was his all-purpose, universal word. He usually hyphenated it: 'Oh, that shit-kid won't do it'; 'What's wrong with the shit-car? Won't start?'; 'Where's the shit-builder?' He used it so often that it became meaningless. The lesser swear-words had no appeal for him: he never said *hell* or *damn* or *sod it*. When things went badly wrong, he used the Russian word *pizdat*, which means 'cunt'. It came in two formats. 'Pizdat', with equal stress on each syllable, signified his disgust at (for instance) a badly swept stage, or overcooked salmon. 'Piz-dat!', with the second syllable almost spat out, was meant to draw blood. A bad dancer was piz-*dat*. A slow ticket-clerk was piz-*dat*. I was both pizdat and piz-*dat*! at various times. You can put a lot into that word and you can get a lot out of it. Rudolf liked it.

15

Only One Way Out

The summer of 1991 was coming to its end when we flew back to Vienna. (As usual, I took the fax machine and the folding motorbike and several other awkward bits of luggage.) Rudolf had concerts lined up in various European cities. To an outsider, his future looked rich.

He was even giving interviews, something he had never done on the British tour. He had a permanent fear that the English language might betray him. It was one thing to dance with Miss Piggy on *The Muppets*, and quite another to appear on prime-time television on *The Terry Wogan Show*. The British tour needed publicity, yet Rudolf had turned Wogan down flat. Too risky. He disliked the rambling, unpredictable nature of chat-shows. He liked to make short, clean-cut statements. If he was talking to someone face-to-face, he ended the sentence with the word 'so', as a full stop: 'We'll meet on Li Galli – so.' If it was a friend, when the talk ended there would be a kiss. Man or woman, the kiss was always on the lips. If it was a phone conversation he ended it with the words, 'Be well.' Nothing more. Never any rabbiting on about lots-of-love-to-your-wife: that was babble. He said, 'Be well,' and hung up. Gossiping with friends was safe. Talking to journalists was not, and he had learned to avoid it. He told of an occasion in the sixties when a play about homosexuality was running in London's West End. This was a daring development, and the Press was as interested in the audience as it was in the play. Rudolf saw the play. During the interval he went to the lavatory. A journalist came in, stood nearby, and slowly realized there might be a story next to him. 'Aren't you Rudolf Nureyev?' he said.

'Not at the moment,' Rudolf said briskly, and stopped the interview in its tracks.

Now that he was launching his new career, he needed publicity. He still didn't find interviews easy. You could sense his relief when he got to the end of each answer without stumbling: his voice always smacked the last word hard, as if to say: *Got you!* It was another little victory over the English language. The war, of course, went on.

So the public view of Nureyev was being polished up, and it may even have been what Rudolf believed. The private picture was less attractive, and I was growing tired of turning a blind eye to it.

I had learned to ignore the merely seedy side of his existence: the stained and grubby clothing he preferred to wear; the porn videos and the tattered packets of condoms in his battered hand-luggage; the intolerance and the penny-pinching and the tantrums. I reckoned that such things went with the territory. Others just couldn't be ignored; things like paying the masseur in Vienna. He did what Rudolf asked him to do, and then told me his fee was 5,000 Austrian schillings – about $500. Far too much, I said. The man shook his head. 'If I had known what sort of job your boss wanted, I wouldn't have agreed to do it. I know who he is, so let's just settle this and forget it.'

I had to borrow some of the money from Moser. When Rudolf learned of the price he was slightly shocked, but not for long. After all, Moser had paid. Rudolf shrugged it off. I found it impossible to forget. My job description didn't include collecting money to pay for Rudolf's sexual pleasures, especially when the price was half my monthly salary. I had already told him I thought I wasn't being paid enough. He disagreed. That was another thing I couldn't forget. We were deadlocked, and since Rudolf would never give in, there was only one way out that I could see.

Infinitesimally, day by day, his body was shrinking. Twelve hours sleep was not enough. The audiences at his concerts noticed that he was thin, but his vigour disguised the true effects of the disease until one day when the rewards of conducting failed to match the demands that it made, and his body simply quit.

We'd gone to Paris, and the nights were getting chilly. Rudolf didn't feel well. As usual he dreaded getting a chest infection. He wore his scarf-shawl tightly wrapped around his throat.

A bunch of dance people, many of them ballerinas or choreographers (Kenneth Macmillan was one) and all of them close friends, invited him to a party. It was several flights up, there was no lift, and the staircase was one of those typically Parisian structures that's almost spiral. Rudolf couldn't walk up it. He was too weak.

We stood and looked at each other. I didn't feel sorry for him; compassion was irrelevant. This was Nureyev, and we lived by Nureyev's standards. How to overcome? That was the question; the only question.

He put his hand out and grasped my wrist, and I grasped his wrist, so that we made a Roman handshake.

'Run up the stairs,' he said.

I took as much of his weight on that arm as I could and we went up the stairs like one man. His feet moved but it was my strength that carried his body. We didn't stop until we reached the door. He straightened his clothes, put his head up, pressed the buzzer and in we went. I was still quietly wheezing. He was sparkling.

It was all a matter of shepherding his resources: the sort of thing he'd done for performances all his life. He might feel lousy all day, but when it mattered, he turned on the brilliance. He had a couple of glasses of champagne and he made the party fizz with chat and laughter. We stayed until one or two in the morning – very late for him. When we got home he was so exhausted I had to help him into the apartment.

The way he behaved in Paris was admirable. The way he behaved in Varese was cheap and nasty.

Varese is north of Milan. Rudolf was there to conduct a concert. He was in bed, resting before the performance, when Benito Fusco and his wife arrived. He didn't want to meet them. He knew why they had come: to collect payment for the work on Li Galli. He gave me an envelope, and I took it down to the hotel lobby. Before Benito had finished counting the money his wife was shaking her head.

I took it back to Rudolf. That was something I would normally never have done; but Benito had been good to me. I said, 'It's not enough, Rudolf.'

'That's all I have,' he said. We both knew this wasn't true. A phone call to Luigi, or a fax to New York, would easily have raised the difference between what he had and what he owed. The truth was he didn't care. He'd got what he wanted. He was indifferent to other people's needs. This was Nureyev at his worst: selfish and dishonest, lacking even the courage to face the people he had shortchanged.

I went down and told the Fuscos. I felt sorry for them, and ashamed of Nureyev. We all knew there was nothing more to be done.

The next time I met them was on a cold, wet January morning in 1993, in Paris. They had come to the Palais Garnier for the funeral service. We went by coach to the cemetery. Everyone was sad and sombre; but afterwards, as the coach took us back to the city, a natural reaction set in. People began remembering events and anecdotes. Benito asked, 'Did you always get paid, Blue?'

I said I did. Sometimes late, but I got paid.

'You're the only one,' he said. He laughed, and a lot of others laughed too. There was no bitterness, because it was too late for bitterness, but there was no lack of candour, either. Nureyev abused his celebrity status to get what he wanted on the cheap. He died worth many millions. Greatness and meanness existed side by side. Probably even Nureyev couldn't explain it. He was what he was.

September 1991, in Milan. Rudolf should have been consolidating his career as a conductor. Instead he was planning a dance tour of Australia. Or rather, others were planning the tour and he was reluctantly agreeing.

We were in Luigi's flat. Michael Edgley, an Australian impresario, had just flown in. They had one evening to pin down this tour. 'We need to call some dancers *now*,' Edgley said.

'Going to be a shit tour.'

'No, no, Rudolf. It'll be great.'

'They're going to be shit venues.'

'Believe me, Rudolf. They'll be great venues.'

The truth was that Rudolf didn't want to perform in big theatres. He wanted to dodge the worst of the critics' flak by appearing only in small theatres. This was the British tour all over again. Part of Rudolf didn't want to go, didn't even want to talk about it. He named Charles Jude and Evelyn Desutter as the two classical dancers he wanted as principals. With that agreed, they began discussing Edgley's list of other dancers. He worked fast, ticking this name, crossing off that. Then he suggested a European ballerina. 'What about X?'

'Probably a good fuck,' Rudolf said. The room was silent. Rudolf was obviously bored, but it had been difficult to set up this meeting, and Edgley had just arrived from the other side of the world. Rudolf's joke fell flat. Edgley got the discussion moving again. They reached a decision on X and on a couple of other dancers, and then Edgley said, 'What about this Latin American boy?'

'Ah, he *is* a good fuck,' Rudolf said. Perfect timing. Everyone laughed. Once more the meeting was off the rails but Rudolf didn't care. The discussion had gone on too long, it had become too heavy, he couldn't resist sabotaging it. That was his mission in life: to take weight and make it light.

The question remains: why did he agree to dance in Australia when his conducting career was just taking off? Partly it was money. Nureyev always found it hard to resist an extra dollar. Partly it was because he still got a kick out of dancing, and to hell with the critics. And there was yet another reason. Dr Canesi's drugs were losing the battle. Rudolf was trying to pack as much as possible into his remaining time on earth.

Rudolf had told me I was going with him to Australia. I certainly wanted to go: Jane was there. (We married in 1995.) Michael Edgley had other ideas. Rudolf was the maestro, but Edgley signed the cheques. He didn't want me. I didn't go.

170

Nevertheless, Rudolf wanted me to continue as his PA. Doing what? Painting window-frames? Sweeping up the mail and throwing it away? Checking the thermostat in the apartment at the Dakota? Hanging around, underpaid, waiting for him to return? I'd hung around too many places, for too long, in the past year. And who was to say that Rudolf would return? He was dying of AIDS. The party was over.

'Don't get trapped with anybody,' Rudolf had told Mukhamedov. 'Follow your own nose.'

The rich and famous are not like Nureyev. They have families, they live on estates, they entertain on the grand scale. If I was to go on doing this sort of job, I still had a lot to learn. A school in London ran a six-week course in modern international butlering. Today's butler is not pear-shaped and portly, like P.G. Wodehouse's Beach at Blandings Castle. Today's butler needs to be fit and fast on his feet, and to know everything from bodyguards to prop-erty management, while serving wine and coping with drunks in between. It sounded like the right sort of training for me.

Rudolf couldn't get his mind around butlering. 'Why are you doing this charm school? You don't need to. You do thing very well. You're good for me.' But when he saw that my mind was made up, he said, 'Follow your nose. Enjoy.'

On 3 October 1991, we were back in Vienna. He was in bed in a hotel, wrapped up, just as he'd been in Cleveland, Ohio, in October 1990 – the hotel-towel turban, the scarf-shawl, the Mickey Mouse sweatshirt. The difference was that there was less of him to wrap up.

I said, 'I'm going to the airport now.' For the first and last and only time, I kissed him on the lips.

That was the kiss he gave when he said farewell to

friends, men or women. Never on the cheek; always on the lips. After twelve months, I reckoned we were friends. I also reckoned that the chances were we would never meet again.

This was the moment he realized that I really was going. 'Oh well,' he said. 'Have a flight.' It was his odd way of wishing me a good flight. He looked at me rather strangely: a serious, slightly puzzled expression. He was probably thinking: *Why has Blue kissed me? Oh well.* . . .

Time to go.

Rudolf Nureyev died in Paris on 6 January 1993.

He was a heroic individual, both for good and for bad. He lived his life to the full, and he never cared what the rest of the world thought of his way of living – unless someone got in his way and wasted his time. 'Too slow,' I hear him say, when I miss an opportunity. Life is measured in seconds, in fractions of seconds. Once they're wasted they never return.

Index

AIDS, 35, 104, 112, 119, 130, 146, 170
Arias, Robert ('Tito'), 89
Ashton, Sir Frederick, 84, 91
Astaire, Fred, 142
Australia, 169–70

Barnardo's, 12
Baryshnikov, Mikhail, 70, 137
Bernstein, Leonard, 35, 45, 78
Bolshoi, 116
Brind, Bryony, 49
British tour, 109–22
Bruhn, Erik, 83–4
Burton, Richard, 82

Canesi, Dr Michel, 93, 112, 146
Capri, 133, 146
Chichikoff, 131
Churchill, Sir Winston, 89
Cleveland, Ohio, 25, 27–32
CNN, 80
Columbia Artists, 24, 38, 103
Concorde, 103
Covent Garden, 92, 139

Dakota, the, 35–45, 97–108
Death in Venice, 50, 123
Desutter, Evelyn, 49, 111, 117, 170
de Warren, Robert, 47–8

Diaghilev, 132
Don Quixote, 106

Edgley, Michael, 169–70
Endeavor (yacht), 21

Fedatov, André, 113
Fonteyn, Margot, 66, 75, 84, 87–93, 95, 124, 162, 164
François, Douce, 59
Fusco, Benito, 137, 155, 168

Gielgud, Sir John, 82
Gosling, Maude, 92, 114, 145, 161
Grand Saline beach, 78–9
Grossman, Andrew, 24, 38, 82, 86
Guillem, Sylvie, 49

Hubener, Wilhelm & Lydia, 149–52

Isaacs, Jeremy, 139

Jersey, 12
Jude, Charles, 49, 111, 117, 170

Keama (yacht), 23, 159
Kennedy, Bobby, 91
Kennedy, John, 76–7

Kennedy, Tessa, 114
KGB, 162
Khrushchev, 136
King and I, The, 18, 37, 78
Kirov Ballet, 94, 136–7
Kruger, Jeff, 109

La Banane, 12, 14, 76, 81
La Scala, 49–53
Le Corsaire, 113
Leesburg, Virginia, 107–8
Lesson The, 111
Li Galli, 126, 129–43, 153–64

Macmillan, Kenneth, 167
Madonna, 104
Magic Flute, The, 150
Marguerite and Armand, 91
Marx Brothers, 142
Massine, Leonarde, 132–4
Milan, 47–53, 169–70
Milanese risotto: recipe, 137
Monroe, Marilyn, 89
Moor's Pavanne, The, 111
Moser, Dr Franz, 145, 150
Mukhamedov, Irek, 114, 147, 171
Muppet Show, The, 139, 165

Nijinsky, 158
Nureyev, Rudolf
  first meeting with, 14–15
  physical description of, 17, 42–3, 78
  nightsweats, 30
  world record for curtain calls, 31
  as maestro, 31
  can't resist slapping ass, 33
  throws punch when challenged, 36
  is semi-literate, 38
  is tightfisted with house-
  keeping costs, 40, 156
  sudden fits of rage, 44
  must have tea, 48
  directs *Nutcracker* at La Scala, 49
  has strong antipathies, 50, 139
  never signs contract, 55
  bans girlfriends on premises, 56
  cuts salary, 56
  irrational impatience, 59
  the 'pen move', 61
  takes AZT pills, 62, 93
  hates flying, 62, 65, 86–7, 103
  love of solitude, 67, 130
  ends discussion if opposed, 68
  refuses to spend despite huge earnings, 69–71
  uncomfortable with money, 72–3
  plans career as conductor, 78
  explosive fury when frustrated, 80–1, 85, 100, 132, 141, 147, 159
  is terrible driver, 82
  his unique achievements, 82–3
  his long-term lovers, 83–4
  fantasy of marrying Margot Fonteyn, 89
  abiding affection for Margot Fonteyn, 92
  injures knee in fall, 94
  always needs hard massage, 97
  problems with banks, 100
  schoolyard humour, 104
  identified as HIV-positive, 105
  pessimism re. British tour, 109

collapses in Edinburgh, 111
fear of AIDS, 112
belief in purpose of dance, 116
despair and rage when meal is late, 121
insists stage be properly swept, 124
kicks dancer and is sued, 126
virtual recluse on island, 129
denies 'leap to freedom' at defection, 136
enjoys Milanese risotto, 137
taste in humour, 142
belief that 'work conquers all', 143
flaunts HIV condition, 147
sensitive to ridicule, 148
success as conductor, 151
can't resist pinching ass, 153
indifference to dirty clothes, 154
gives free dance lessons, 157
his incurable distrust, 163
plays on image of coarse Tartar, 163
seedy existence contrasts with glamorous image, 166
too weak to walk upstairs, 157
shortchanges builder, 168
deflates serious discussion, 170
puzzled by parting, 171
Nureyev and Friends, 38, 95, 101, 104, 111
Nutcracker, 49–53

Ocean Leopard (yacht), 13, 15, 17, 23
Onassis, Jackie, 75–7
O'Toole, Peter, 81

Palais Auersperg, 146, 149–50
Palais Garnier, 49, 86, 169
Paris, 55–63
Paris Opéra, 58, 86, 143
Penny Howard, 156–7
Pignotti, Luigi, 24, 50–1, 102, 114, 139, 164, 169
Positano, 133
Potts, Wallace, 84, 102

'Randolph Neveroff', 158
Raymonda, 139

St Barts, 12–13, 65–95
Sleeping Beauty, 113
Solymosi, Zoltan, 114
Sunderland Empire, 109–10
Suzanne, Marie, 140–1

Tracy, Robert, 35–7, 40–1, 69, 84–5, 102, 105

Varese, 168
Verona, 123–8
Vidal, Gore, 154, 158
Vienna, 145–52, 165–72
von Karajan, Herbert, 78

Wembley, 114
Wilde, Oscar, 153
Wogan, Terry, 165